THE VEIL OF ENTANGLEMENT

CALM ABIDING AND INSIGHT PRACTICE –
AN ACCOUNT OF A JOURNEY

T. J. NICHOLSON

The Veil of Entanglement:
Calm Abiding and Insight Practice – An Account of a Journey
© 2022 T.J. Nicholson

All rights reserved. No part of this publication may be reproduced, stored in a retrieval system, or transmitted in any form or by any means—electronic, mechanical, photocopied, recorded or otherwise—without prior written permission of the publisher, except in the case of brief quotations embodied in critical reviews and certain other noncommercial uses permitted by copyright law.

Published in Canada by TJN Books 2022
www.tjnbooks.ca
ISBN 978-1-7779161-0-7 (hardcover) 978-1-7779161-1-4 (paperback)
Fifth and final printing with refinements – January 2026

Edited with rigour and insight by Michael Kenyon.

Manuscript evaluation by Sarah Chauncey.
Copy edit by Dania Sheldon.
Cover produced by Jan Westendorp of Kato Design & Photo.
Back cover graphic by Gordon Johnson from Pixabay.

 Created with Vellum

Prefatory epigraph from *The Rebel Physicist on the Hunt for a Better Story Than Quantum Mechanics*, Bob Henderson, The New York Times. © 2020 The New York Times Company. All rights reserved. Used under license.

Epigraph to Chapter 9 from *Fearful Symmetry: A Study of William Blake*, Northrop Frye, © 1968. Republished with permission of Princeton University Press; permission conveyed through Copyright Clearance Center, Inc.

Epigraphs to Chapters 10 and 11 from *The Great Code*, Northrop Frye, © 1990, Penguin Books. Republished with permission of HMH Books & Media.

Epigraph to Chapter 12 from *Einstein's God: Albert Einstein's Quest as a Scientist and as a Jew to Replace a Forsaken God*, Robert N. Goldman, Albert Einstein, © 1996. Republished with permission of Rowman & Littlefield Publishing Group, Inc.; permission conveyed through Copyright Clearance Center, Inc.

Epigraph to Chapter 13 from *The Passion of the Western Mind*, Richard Tarnas, © 1991, Random House. Republished with permission of Hill Nadell Literary Agency.

Epigraphs to Chapters 14 and 15 from *The Order of Time*, Carlo Rovelli, copyright © 2017 by Adelphi Edizioni SpA, Milano. Translation copyright © 2018 by Simon Carnell and Erica Segre. Used by permission of Riverhead, an imprint of Penguin Publishing Group, a division of Penguin Random House LLC. All rights reserved. And from *The Order of Time* by Carlo Rovelli published by Allen Lane. Copyright © Adelphi Edizioni SpA, Milano 2017. Reprinted by permission of Penguin Books Limited.

Excerpts from *Seeing That Frees*, Rob Burbea, © 2014, Hermes Amāra Publications: Newton Abbot, Devon. Republished with permission of Hermes Amāra Foundation.

Excerpts from *Pointing Out the Great Way: The Stages of Meditation in the Mahāmudrā Tradition*, Daniel P. Brown, © 2006. Reprinted by arrangement with Wisdom Publications, Inc., wisdompubs.org.

ACKNOWLEDGEMENTS

Everything I have learned about calm-abiding concentration and insight practice came my way through the unreserved generosity of my teacher, Daniel P. Brown. An eminent clinician, researcher, and scholar, he is as at home translating ancient Tibetan texts as he is advancing the frontiers of contemplative neuroscience. He is a vigilant guardian of precious human traditions of contemplative practice he has dedicated his life to cherishing, practising, and propagating. As a teacher, he has been simultaneously demanding and deeply caring. His patience with me—expressed often enough as impatience—was stoical. He always taught me where I was, even as I wandered, delayed, and resisted. Not a word of this book would have been set down but for him. His own book, *Pointing Out the Great Way*, served as a guiding reference for me in the writing of this one. All the practices I describe in this book I learned from Dan, and I use much of the same vocabulary in describing them here as he used in teaching them to me. Even as this is an otherwise original work of my own, there will be echoes in it of the hours he spent teaching me. The presentation, commentary, interpretation, and errors are all my own.

Susan Mickel, an accomplished teacher in her own right, combines professional credentials in neurology and psychology with a practice steeped in the traditions of both the East and the West. She has been and continues to be gracious enough to take my calls and wise enough to attend to very little of what I have to say, but always the right very little. With her exacting eye and the breadth of her knowledge, she challenged me to clarify both my thinking and my writing. Susan teaches directly from experience, and she inspires by embodying the practice.

George Protos, closely taught and trained by Dan Brown, and himself an exemplar of light-hearted and intelligent practice, has accompanied me from the first retreat I witlessly wandered into. A gifted and dedicated teacher, he is responsible for a turn of phrase that broke the first and most imposing logjam I faced in my practice. He continues to land perfectly placed coinages when I turn to him for his counsel.

None of these teachers stands on ceremony, and all have had the good humour and forbearance to entertain my improvisations as I recast the traditions in terms that were both accurate renderings and meaningful to me. They unhesitatingly teach me both from where I am coming from, and from where I am going to.

I am gigantically grateful to my fellow students who spoke openly of their frustrations and joys—expressed often enough as frustrations—with calm-abiding concentration and insight practice, thereby sharing with me not just the intimacies of their journeys but also the inspiration of their dogged perseverance.

T. J. Nicholson
January 2022

THE VEIL OF ENTANGLEMENT

CONTENTS

Preface xiii
Introduction xix

PART I
PRELIMINARIES

1. Motivation 3
2. Tools 9

PART II
CALM ABIDING

3. Capacities 29
4. Placing and Staying 37
5. Refining and Intensifying 55
6. Releasing and Spaciousness 73
7. Knowingness 95
8. Practice 109

PART III
INSIGHT

9. Text 123
10. Stages 133
11. Insight 141
12. Self 157
13. Phenomena 185
14. Time 203

PART IV
RETROSPECT AND PROSPECT

15. Practice 213

Dedication 223
Afterword 225
In Memoriam Daniel P. Brown 227
Annotated Bibliography 231
Notes 237

Schrödinger coined a term—"entanglement"—for the way ... the wave functions of any two interacting objects, including observer and observed, get wove [*sic*] into one.... Entanglement could be responsible for keeping objective reality behind a veil.

— Bob Henderson in *The New York Times*

PREFACE

About the book

In the midst of a challenging, absorbing, stressful, and chronically overtime career in technology in which I could not have been more happily engaged, I took myself off to a coastal retreat for a week of relaxation and rejuvenation. I expected that the attendant program, billed as an introduction to meditation, would not interfere with my planned indolence, and that the week would pass by serenely enough. I envisioned myself lying about on cushions, soaking in hot tubs, having my meals prepared for me, and falling asleep to the sound of the ocean.

On the opening evening, the teacher, Daniel P. Brown, described a set of ancient practices that, he said, would bring me face-to-face with the nature of my mind, the very mind in which I felt so vitally enmeshed. At his words, an old longing stirred in me. In the depths, a compass needle silently wheeled round and settled, expectantly, upon the pull of something vast, trackless, and perfectly still.

Until then, it had not occurred to me that I might have been so suited up in my life that I had become estranged from the stark nakedness of my own nature. I sought none of these practices, but I could not walk away from the entrancing prospect they offered. So, foreign as they were to me, I set out on my journey with them.

THIS BOOK was written for those least likely to come to these practices in their usual contexts. It was written for coders and mechanics, builders and engineers, scientists and tinkerers. It was written for makers and technicians of any description, in the belief that the characteristics of the type—appreciation for detail, intransigence with respect to evidence, promiscuity with respect to experience, ebullient curiosity—are fertile preconditions for a revitalized practice of introspection.

This is a handbook meant to inspire the reader to explore the practices described herein, and to guide the reader in learning to learn them. This doubling of the learning task is necessary for those of us who find the presumption and credulity of both contemporary and traditional teaching and writing on the topic of concentration and insight practice unwelcoming. The book provides an introduction to and an overview of the path of practice in terms as unencumbered as possible by overlays of culture, tradition, and belief so that the reader may come to appreciate in its essentials the startling proposition at stake. Even as the text is instructive, the primary intent is to survey the path of practice, providing the reader with a clear idea of its scope and progress.

I describe this as a handbook because as much as you may be able to learn from it, you will require a teacher adept in both practising and teaching these practices to bring them fully to life. Accordingly, along the way will be advice on what to expect of a teacher, as well as at what point in your practice and in what ways a teacher can be helpful. In time, interested readers may find it worthwhile to turn to more conventional teaching sources, on the lookout for what they will then be able to recognize as the gems nestled amongst the glittering display. This is the spirit in which I was taught, and it is my fondest hope to pass this opportunity on to as many others as are inclined to listen.

The territory I am treading here is sprawling and august. It is a monumental expression in the larger human endeavour—a living, continually elaborating universe of ideas and practices. It is, in one instance, the cherished cultural treasure of an entire nation harried into diaspora. It is a self-fulfilling phenomenon in the midst of which an untutored voice can seem an affront, especially when the field is littered with luminaries, emissaries, and incarnations, the genuine custodians of the letter and the lineage. My intent in this book is in no way to attempt to improve upon teachings that have come down the ages and proven themselves over and over again. I have no qualifications other than that I spent a decade trying to learn to practise. My intent is to describe the practical experience that allowed me to make my way into and through a fraction of these teachings and practices, despite finding them —in my sceptical, secular context—in an idiom with which I had no rapport.

I can only write from my predicament—my lineage, if you like. As a Westerner, I live in the wake of convulsive reformations and revolutions, and the litany of atrocities that was the twentieth century. In the face of this inheritance, the only conscionable stance I can adopt is an ironic one. Too many lives have been ground up in violence and horror to abandon the principles for which they paid. Specifically, direct experience is primary, and every text is an interpretation; none is revealed, none is privileged. Upon these principles, power is to be held to account.

What created an opening for me with these practices is that there is a similarly radical stance at the heart of the traditions themselves. It's just not put about too widely, as it's at odds with the authoritarian aims of orthodoxy.

IN WRITING about my experience as his student, I mean to honour Dan Brown and his way of teaching; in this book, when I say, "I was taught," I mean, "As I was taught by Dan." All the same, this book is an interpretive description, a personal one based on my experience of these teachings, and not a reference for them. Along the way, I made adaptations that enabled me to develop my practice in ways that were authentic for me. These recastings are central to the story I have to tell. Otherwise, I have done all I can to be as faithful to these teachings as my experience, my recall, and the sources available to me allow.

I offer this as an unsanctioned student essay on learning to practise, written by a student who is still learning to practise, so it is subjective and provisional. It downplays distorting descriptions of results, let alone benefits, and it requires attention and application on the part of the reader.

This book is also burdened by the knowledge that I would only ever write the one, so at the reader's expense, I have stuffed everything into it. That's an admission, not an apology: everything I've written about here has meant the world to me. It is an account of how I heard these teachings, how I organized and interpreted them to make them work for myself, and how I still tell them to myself as my practice unfolds in my life. So it is written in an instructive form: this is the sound of my older self telling my younger self the story I wish I had heard much earlier in life than I did.

THAT STORY, THEN, is one of a journey, the journey from distraction to composure through the practice of calm abiding, and from unknowing to awareness through the practice of insight. Along the way, questions of both "being" and "knowing" arise and play out with intricacy and delicacy.

For the general reader, the key to reading this book is to recognize that it is, as it announces itself to be, a work of fiction. It is a work of fiction in the sense that it tells a story, in the sense that it is the story of the telling of that story, and in the sense that there is, in any case, no such thing as nonfiction. As a story chiefly about the reactive self, it provokes the reactive self, with the unfortunate consequence that, should you take the second person to be yourself, it becomes all too easy to get arrested right there by that most ready and comforting of wardens.

For the reader already in search of what the book has to say, it is, ultimately, a story of natural magic: a practice of inspiration, invocation, and transformation leading to liberation and compassion should the reader care to engage.

I CAME HERE by accident and have been made nothing but welcome. What has been put in my hands has made for the most extraordinary adventure of my life. Everything I have to say here I offer with profound gratitude to my teachers and to the lineage of which they are the embodiment. The only way I can give back is to bring practice into my life in a way that is faithful both to them and to myself. My own journey was much more of a muddle than the trajectory I've laid out here, but as it progressed, it did clarify and organize itself to align with the teachings, my temperament, and what have turned out to be my abilities. I offer this account in the hope that, for the sake of practice, it might inspire other hearts and minds like mine to find their own way to these teachings.

About the author

I wrote this book at a time in my life when I had become keenly aware of the world of care, kindness, generosity, and love my parents bestowed upon me. In honour of them and all the gifts they gave me, not least my life, I've chosen a pen name that combines the initials of my father's first names with my mother's family name.

INTRODUCTION

The intent of the practices described in this book is nothing less than to liberate you by revealing to you, in your own direct experience, the nature of your mind.

If you think you already know your own mind, you might want to examine both those verbs. We maintain a privileged stance of knowing based upon a flow of experience that comes to us exclusively through the fisheye lens of the thinking mind, without realizing that this lens, for all its dazzling acuity, is also a distorting filter. The cinematic splendour of thought and emotion, of memory and of dream, is not the whole picture; from where are those projections beaming?

This question of the nature of mind has been at the centre of human inquiry from time immemorial. It has been driven as much by restless curiosity as by a sense of something ineffable beckoning from just beyond the fringes of human experience, a sense that being has a ground. It has swirled about with varying degrees of disruption under the auspices of philosophy and religion in their crude and refined forms, ever vexing, never resolving.

Traditions of contemplative practice—the contemplation of the mind by the mind—meant to investigate this question have descended from both domains across cultures and across the centuries. Amongst them, the Buddhist traditions have evolved contemplative practices of uncommon detail and precision, including an enduring pedagogy that lays out a complete path of practice leading the practitioner to a direct, experiential encounter with the nature of mind.

However, for those of us of a sceptical, secular disposition, these practices are not easy to appreciate, encased as they are within the orthodoxies and cultural encrustations of the Buddhist traditions flourishing in the world today. The intent in this book is to distill a description of a fraction of these practices out of their traditional settings, to make them available for both inspection and practice in a secular context. Since this distillation is across a number of Buddhist traditions, I'll refer to them hereafter simply as "the traditions," to minimize both appropriation and affiliation.

What I have written here neither requires nor assumes any prior experience with contemplative practice. It sets aside enthusiasm in favour of a detailed, structured, practical approach—first, to uncovering the concentration abilities native to mind, and second, to establishing them in an enduring and serviceable way in the hands of the practitioner. Whereupon the insight practices are presented not as exotic experiences in some transcendent domain but as encounters with natural mind, available to direct, awake experience.

For the contemporary sceptic, these foundational practices can stand on their own, independent of the traditions in which they are embedded. Undertaking them requires no dispensation from authority, no subscription to particular beliefs. You may also be relieved to know that they depend in no way upon seclusion, a vegetarian diet, or celibacy.

Introduction

The arrangement of the concentration practices as a prerequisite to insight practice is traditional, but don't let anything about the syllabus dictate how your path unfolds. I know of gifted practitioners who listened attentively but with a touch of impatience to the concentration practices, arrived at the insight practices without a lot of difficulty, and realized them almost casually, as though they were second nature.

I, on the other hand, had to make my way painstakingly, step by step, and it's that incremental journey I've recounted here.

The traditions propose that the nature of mind is not something unknown to discover. Rather, it's something we live in the midst of to uncover, something we already know but from which we have become estranged. So the journey through these practices is framed as a journey of liberation: calm-abiding concentration practice is intended to gain freedom *for* yourself, insight practice to gain freedom *from* yourself. It's a journey of liberation from the veil of entanglement, that knotted fist of unmediated reactivity organized around the self, the self in which we are entangled and which so separates us from the ground of being.

WE'LL START WITH an intuitive notion of reactivity: those positive and negative emotional responses of attraction and aversion we experience as arising pretty much on their own, rooted in our hopes and desires, and in our anxieties and fears, the two not always easy to differentiate from one another. Mostly unnoticed, but just as consequential, are the less prominent neutral emotional responses such as thoughtless indifference or mindless obliviousness. Consider that, at some level, we notice everything in experience, but these neutral responses dismiss much before it even has time to rise into awareness. Reactivity is at work in what we discard from our experience early on.

All these emotional responses, however, are at the tail end of an intricate and subtle chain of reactions that precede them. The blank slate of direct experience—experience before anything has been made of it—passes through a cascade of reactive filters as we become aware of it, a cascade that makes nonsense of the conceit of objectivity. The senses impose their specific modes on it. The cultures and histories we live in narrate it to us. Our characters and the phases and conditions of our lives cast it all in an individual context.

Above all, the experience of life and death will come to you in the unique incarnation of the life and death of the mortal body you were born into, determined by its constitution, its capacities and frailties, its clamorous sensuality.

Even the way we communicate experience, to ourselves and to one another, is a reaction, a coercion of experience into linguistic structures that not only edit experience into their own fictions but also construct distinct human worlds and world views that encode contrasting, and usually conflicting, assumptions and expectations.

While you can start with your own intuitive notion of what is meant by reactivity, as you read this book and practise, be prepared for the scope of the word to widen as your own direct experience reveals to you, in ever greater detail and subtlety, the breadth and power of reactivity as it moves to shape all of experience. The good news is that every such movement is an opportunity for liberation.

I AM USING the words "liberation" and "freedom" interchangeably in this text, and by them, I mean release from entanglement. While freedom is the outcome of both concentration and insight practice, it's a very different freedom in each case.

The freedom sought in concentration practice, freedom for yourself, is the freedom from the entangling bonds of your reactivity. It is only circumstantial freedom, enduring—when it does—only on the cushion. It is ephemeral respite, creating the conditions of mind in which you can productively engage in insight practice.

The freedom sought in insight practice, freedom from yourself, is the more profound freedom from the reactive grip of the self. The goal is a sustained and ambient liberty throughout your life, a transformation of how you are in the world. In both cases, I use the word "liberation" to mean the process of becoming free, all the freeing up you do until your freedom is self-sustaining.

The nature of knowledge

In addition to open-minded curiosity, an expansive attitude toward knowledge is required to undertake and understand these practices.

The much-maligned tradition of secular scepticism in the West—all of its collateral damage notwithstanding—has brought unprecedented rights and freedoms, in particular the right to self-determination and freedom of expression, to anyone lucky enough to be born into its world and temperamentally adapted to living with the chaos and doubt this world entails. Embedded in the foundation of the accompanying empiricism is the great prejudice that subjective investigation yields results that are not externally verifiable and are therefore suspect. Implicit in this ban on the subjective is an assumption not just that everything knowable is externally verifiable, but also that it can be articulated in language, and that this articulation is the transformation of knowledge into an objective form. Equations are the holy of holies in this regard.

But more fundamental to knowing than verification is recognition. Recognition is the ground of knowing, that silent, internal blip on the radar screen of the mind that incites attention, that offers up to the roving mind a flicker of speculation, that coheres a specific possibility out of the infinities in response to the mind's yearning. If knowing is the light of the mind, recognition is the spark of the mind. Recognition is the reason there's something rather than nothing. Verification is what we apply after the fact to confirm what we have first discerned through recognition. What we call knowledge has as both its roots and its durability subjective recognition, that intimate moment when knowing comes to light.

You already know this experience. You already know it as something that occurs, rather than as something you do. You are already familiar with the moment of integration it entails. All of concentration and insight practice turns on this one gesture of the mind. Recognition is the sole guide to practice.

I AM USING the word "recognition" in this text in two ways. The first use I make of the word is the conventional one, as "recognition of" something, where recognition elaborates up out of direct experience into conceptual knowledge. But in the context of direct experience—once again, experience before anything has been made of it—I am using recognition as the name of an exclusively non-conceptual capacity of mind, the gesture out of which knowledge arises, both conceptual and non-conceptual. In everyday experience, we do not usually distinguish this unmediated moment in the mind from everything it gives rise to. This non-conceptual capacity of mind is unelaborated recognition, just an elemental movement of mind, and this use of the word "recognition" is uncommon outside of practice.

It is essential to distinguish between these two uses in practice. In the context of concentration practice, recognition typically elaborates into conceptual knowledge. For instance, you will come to recognize the capacities of your mind, making it possible for you to identify and deploy them.

In the context of insight practice, however, recognition does not elaborate. It stays at calm, non-conceptual knowing. Insight.

Unfortunately, the language of description in both contexts is the same; we always speak of recognizing "something." In the case of concentration practice, description of what is recognized is meant to be corroborating, but in the case of insight practice, description is only ever evocative, never accurate, often misleading—yet it's the best we can do from within language. It is up to readers to discern which use of "recognition" is intended, from a combination of the context and their own experience.

In both contexts, knowledge originates in recognition, not in thinking.

But let's be careful. Verification makes knowledge dependable enough to be both generalizable and applicable. Verification is the great destroyer of the tyranny of scholasticism, the tyranny of superstition, the tyranny of revelation. We risk much to profess as knowledge anything that cannot be confirmed outside of individual experience.

So is there such a thing as unprofessable knowledge—knowledge that is neither generalizable, in the sense that it cannot be articulated in language, nor applicable, in the sense that it cannot be put to practical use? Is there knowledge that hangs solely upon recognition and cannot be extended from there to persecute our fellow beings in word or in deed?

Is there knowledge that just is, that eludes any attempt to give voice to it or to wield it? If so, what kind of knowledge would this be, and what would its outcome be?

See for yourself. Concentration and insight practice challenge you to ask these questions of yourself, and to rely upon the gift of recognition in the incontestable field of your own direct experience to respond to them. This is an empirical endeavour, taking the evidence of the mind rather than the evidence of the evident. Whether you learn anything along the way depends intimately on your own authentic experience to corroborate what I have written here. In any case, there is nothing you can do with what you come to know. Which is not to say it won't have its consequences.

A map of the book

Part I introduces the two fundamentals of practice upon which everything to follow is built: why you have come here, and what you can do about it.

Chapter 1 is a tart statement of the motivation that originally drew me to these practices and keeps me coming back to them. If it unfolds for you as it did for me, your motivation will broaden and deepen as this book progresses, and as you and your practice are drawn more intimately into the world. You have quite the journey ahead of you, and without motivation that's woven right into you, the voyage will end up being not much more than a pointless endurance test. As I was taught, if your motivation is sound, everything else will follow. Everything.

Chapter 2 takes you on a meticulous tour of your body to acquaint you with the fine instrument of practice it is. This is the first of many experiential descriptions of practice in the book, and it will introduce you at the outset to the kind of close engagement these practices require.

We are embodied beings, and if your practice becomes detached from this raw fact, you can end up wandering aimlessly. The body is, viscerally, the root of practice.

Part II presents detailed and practical descriptions of six calm-abiding concentration practices that will take you through all the traditional "stages of concentration."

Chapter 3 orients you to the traditional pedagogy on which I have based this presentation of the calm-abiding concentration practices, and it gives you an idea of how practice comes alive in life.

Chapters 4 through 6 take you on the journey through the concentration practice skills themselves, each one incrementally reinforcing the others, all of them worth practising again and again. There are exercises and refinements to explore, and there are practical hints for growing and protecting your practice. Chapter 6 closes with the first in a beautiful sequence of shifts in contemplative perspective that will enable the full potential of practice to flourish. At this point in your journey, you are encouraged to loop back to the beginning of the practices to see how the easefulness of this new perspective refreshes the skills themselves.

Chapter 7 describes a second and pivotal shift in contemplative perspective, the shift to "knowingness," to what's known as the knowing aspect of awareness, from which the insight practices will yield up all they hold. The chapter includes a fairly thorny section on a linguistic framework that will serve us throughout the exploration of the insight practices, but which we will dispense with when the time comes. Once again, you are encouraged to loop back to the beginning of the practices to see how your experience and proficiency with these skills from this new perspective reduce your dependence upon them.

And this is key: at the outset, concentration practice is effortful and disciplined, as you become more and more accustomed to taking responsibility for the state of your mind; but ultimately, the goal is to discover the poise and calm your mind is naturally capable of, eventually leaving explicit concentration practice behind. With practice, calm abiding ends up being a place you just go to with not much more than intention. It takes a bit of work, though, to cultivate this potential.

Chapter 8 returns to the theme of how practice now comes alive in life. While the concentration practices are presented as exercises on the cushion, they have a way also of becoming constructively disruptive of the entangling patterns of your daily life. The chapter closes with an encouragement to deepen your motivation for your practice to come to have real meaning in your life.

The first three chapters of Part III—Chapters 9, 10, and 11—are the most personal and ruminative. They are a prelude to the insight practices, and they recount the accommodations I made with the traditions to be able to undertake these practices with respect and integrity.

Chapter 9 describes a way of reading traditional texts that enabled me to appreciate their wisdom. What were once esoteric and inscrutable books that seemed to come from another age altogether have turned out to comprise a literature in its own right, subtle and elusive to be sure, but enthralling in its own way. To continue the journey with practice beyond the scope of this book, the secular sceptic will need to turn to traditional sources for their original instruction, and with an ear attuned to their idiom.

Chapter 10 outlines the entire path of practice, as the traditions render it, to locate the insight practices within that path and to enable you to recognize its "stages" where they echo throughout the traditional literature upon which you will come to depend.

Chapter 11 expands on the insight practices from the "stages of meditation" section of the path described in Chapter 10 and details the "two truths" framework that gives conceptual life to the whole endeavour. But most importantly, it introduces the notion of a "view" and the way of knowing upon which insight depends. It's here in this chapter that the notion of knowledge that "just is" is brought into the foreground to challenge the dominance of conceptual mind. Your journey with insight practice will turn out to be as much an exploration of "knowing" as it is of "being."

This question of the nature of knowledge then returns in the insight practices themselves, described in Chapters 12, 13, and 14, and each chapter elaborates upon variations of the theme. While the format in these chapters is still instructive, I present these practices here only as descriptions, as signposts to the reader, serving only to show you how to learn to learn. As each chapter progresses, the descriptions get less and less practical and more and more evocative. They are, at best, postcards from a distant shore you may one day travel to and be able to recognize once you set foot.

Chapter 15 is valedictory and gets a little carried away but comes back home in the end to the heart of practice: compassion and conduct.

PART I

PRELIMINARIES

1
MOTIVATION

Why would you turn to such a quest, the quest to encounter the nature of your mind? Because you have been had. Your sensibilities have been pummelled with media narcotics. You are careening from sugar to salt, incrementally overfed in a drip-by-drip process of addiction, huddled over your electronics, thumbing your way through a miracle. The practices described herein require you to distinguish distinctive but subtle qualities of your mind. If you have been hollowed out by commodity and trivialized by convenience, you will have been robbed of a vital sense of discrimination. That's "vital" as in "essential to your life."

Ask yourself how much of your attention is directed where you intend, how much spent examining what you think, how much spent choosing actions rather than simply reacting, how much spent considering your conduct. The first of the concentration practices described here will give you a pretty good idea of how little of your attention has not been stolen away. You are in the midst of a palatial great night with a penlight, lurching from the one little thing it illuminates to another. At a fundamental level, you don't know what you're doing. This is an absurd way to live.

. . .

WHAT'S at stake in this endeavour is the freedom to live as who you truly are. The intent of the calm-abiding concentration practices is to free you from the torrent of unmediated reactivity in which your life is being swept away. The intent of the insight practices is to free you from the grip of the anxious self around which all that reactivity is organized. The recovery of this freedom is in your hands, since you are the one sustaining your own entanglement. When you first begin to practise, just remember this each time you think you don't have the time to sit. Consider what you have lost, and know that the traditions offer you everything you need to regain it through a direct encounter with the nature of your mind.

Beginning with sitting on a cushion, the practices you are about to discover require attention to understand, patience to practise, perseverance to keep alive in your life, and confidence to shield from doubt and all the other hazards of a solitary undertaking. But above all, the survival of your practice depends on your motivation. At the outset, your motivation may be simply to find the peace of mind that will show up in your sitting practice only for brief intervals to begin with, but eventually for longer intervals you will come to treasure. These experiences on the cushion may occasion satisfaction as they lengthen, or frustration when they don't last. Both satisfaction and frustration are impediments to the development of your practice. The antidote for them is to revisit your motivation.

Beginning with self-care makes sense. It's wise to equip and bolster yourself before you set out on a journey. But eventually, to get beyond mere relief, your motivation must evolve into something more profound and durable: self-respect. Become both a gentle caretaker of and a fierce advocate for the being you are, no longer seeking just relief but restoration.

Extend your commitment from the experience of peace of mind to the experience of confidence and dignity. Fight back to clear a space of your own to stand in.

As the first signs of liberation strengthen, your being can start to come up for air, shake off the fog of unknowing, and take in the cleared-out surroundings. The evolution of your motivation in this way will serve you well throughout the concentration practices. By the time you get to the insight practices, it will be obvious to you what more that motivation must become.

Practice

Practice begins as these practices themselves, descriptions spoken by teachers or written about in books like this one. It starts out as a set of instructions and the stories that go with them, stories with no purpose other than to await readers who are open to them. Once you undertake any of these practices, however tentatively or whole-heartedly, practice becomes practising—the allotment of time in your life to step away from the habits of mind and revisit that mind on its own terms, based on the recognition that the mind has breadths and depths you only intuit at this point.

The viability of practice at this precarious moment depends on whether you are moved, however imperceptibly, by the tiny gestures of reconciliation your mind will be making to you. If you are so inclined, this initial foray leads to practice as a daily habit on the cushion, accommodated with everything else in the busyness of your daily life. On-the-cushion practice is an external acknowledgement to yourself, and perhaps to others, that you have made a commitment to this undertaking. It's also the beginning of what will be a patchy process of sticking to that undertaking, neglecting it, wishing you hadn't set yourself up for it, keeping the cushion out of sight to keep it from irritating you, but eventually, resolving to go back to it because something still beckons you. This is a process both of recognizing your loss and of becoming more disciplined.

Once you have some continuity on the cushion, practice starts to permeate your daily life off the cushion as an undercurrent, even as the habits of mind flood back in. An awareness of the mind as you are coming to know it stays in place as a backdrop to all of experience, sometimes vividly, sometimes faintly, sometimes lost in the din, but never far away.

This undercurrent off the cushion and your practice on the cushion then start to foster each other. Most of your daily life turns into practice as you start to recognize in every moment off the cushion the imprint of the mind that has begun to reveal itself to you on the cushion.

This recognition starts to influence the choices you make, choices that are more consistent with and do less damage to your mind as you are coming to know it. In this way, practice shows up in your conduct. You start to live the practice. In time, living this way changes how you are. You become the practice. Practice lifts off the page and makes its way into the world through you, as you.

THIS IS A PRACTICAL WORK. If the practices described herein bring you a measure of freedom, it will be your own doing. Like any quest for freedom, this endeavour can be difficult and disruptive, awkward and uncertain, sure signs you are headed in the right direction. The consequences of this endeavour for your personal happiness are incidental, the blandishments of popular books on contemplative practice notwithstanding.

Along the way, there will be those for whom it will be urgent to be telling you what to believe. Instead, require that the received wisdom re-prove itself in the context of your own direct experience.

With introspection, you are very much on your own. Of the many external supports you may find for practice, none can prevent you from fooling yourself or, if you really put your mind to it, from fooling others. You will continuously have to strike a balance between the creative forces of imagination and inspiration and invocation, and the unflinching arbiter of authenticity: recognition in your own direct experience. Concentration and insight practice will be directed toward disarming thinking and the self by recognizing them for what they are. Without these gravitational centres of life as you have lived it thus far, there is every opportunity for persuasive fabrications to rush in to fill the space. If you succumb to or collude with them, you may well end up betraying yourself.

For these practices to flourish, it would be helpful if, somewhere in the stream of your life, your mind gestured to you, however fleetingly, in a way that was not your doing, and you noticed. If you have read this far, it's likely that it did, and you did. If no such memory resonates for you, these practices can serve as the certain enablers of such an encounter.

Calm-abiding concentration and insight practice offer to anyone willing to apply themselves an experience of mind unavailable by any other natural means. We live in our minds like fish in water, unaware of the nature of the pervasive, transparent, all-enabling medium. We may catch glimpses of that nature in moments of inspiration when the light is just right, but mostly we live out our lives and expire without ever having opened to the realm from which being itself arises. It hardly occurs to us that we might.

2
TOOLS

Fortunately enough, it turns out you already have all the tools you need for concentration and insight practice. You were born with them, in them. You just need to learn to use them with all the delicacy and precision of which they are capable. You will need your whole body, but especially your eyes and your breath, to serve as the channels through which your mind will reveal itself to you. You will need imagination to free yourself when you become mired, and vigilance to bring yourself down to earth when you go astray. And you will need the incontestable field of your own direct experience to confirm everything you come to know.

Body

One of the first things you will be taught is to compose your body to facilitate and sustain a sitting practice. The most moving images of contemplatives through the ages show them in attitudes of composure and stillness, to which we may instinctively attribute a quality of sleepiness, if not cessation. But the posture required for sitting practice is instead a continuously active and alert one, a sustained balance of stimulation and effortlessness.

The traditional description of the classical cross-legged posture has its own rules and regulations, but you may find that a careful investigation of the ways in which your own body is naturally capable of stability, ease, and poise will not only provide a more natural description, it will also walk you through what you can practicably do to set up such a posture for yourself.[1] However obvious and flat-footed the following investigation may seem, try following along and attending with care to the dynamics of this body and everything it's doing for you that you take for granted.

Muscle

To begin with, stand up straight with your feet together, flat on the ground, your hands at rest at your sides, looking directly ahead of you. This may seem an uneventful posture with not much to notice about it, but you should be able to notice that one of the things you are doing is not falling over. If the mechanics of not falling over don't seem remarkable to you, close your eyes, keeping your feet right together. When you remove the governing coordination of vision, you will feel the incessant, minute machinations of your musculature as it works autonomously—and a little frantically—to keep you upright. The wobbling you experience with your eyes closed results from that musculature, abandoned by the usual speed-of-light guidance provided by vision, having to switch autopilots to the equally sensitive but more sluggish mechanical balance in your inner ear.

Pay attention to the character of what you experience when you close your eyes. A background swarm of muscular activity you were largely unaware of supplants the relaxed liberty of the mind, and you instead become narrowly involved in the details of keeping yourself from falling over. Open your eyes again, and attend to the restoration of your accustomed mental expanse. In your sitting posture, it will be the unnoticed business of the intricate web of your musculature to maintain for you a flawless background of physical poise.

Bone

Now, once again looking directly ahead, first stand with your feet together, then shift your stance so that your feet are about shoulder width apart. Unlike in the first exercise, the difference you will notice this time is one of increased, rather than decreased, stability. The structure of your body has taken over from the musculature of your body to some extent, so that a static physical component of support, provided by the beams and girders of your skeleton, has relieved your musculature of having continuously and actively to man its guy wires, at least for side-to-side motion.

Pay attention to this quality of increased stability, the corresponding tensions it relieves, the sense of it having an intrinsic soundness to impart without you having to do anything. Consider that your body in itself has the ability to follow its own plumb lines to stability.

Mass

Now sit on a chair with a cushion to keep your hips a little higher than your knees, your knees bent at ninety degrees, your feet flat on the ground about shoulder width apart, your back straight and unsupported by the back of the chair, your shoulders dropped and back so the chest is open, looking directly ahead of you. Choose a position for your hands— together, palms up, one hand resting in the other, thumbs gently touching each other, forming an oval, lightly against your body just below the navel; or apart, palms down on your knees—that best supports your ability to keep the chest open and the hands at rest at the same time as the arms remain poised. You should now be doing about half as much not falling over as when you were standing, since more of you is being supported directly by gravity.

Our usual appreciation of gravity is resentment for the way it weighs us down and breaks our stuff, but for a sitting practice, gravity turns out to be actively benevolent. It holds up the lower half of your body, and it provides you with a firm base upon which to poise the rest of it. To get a clearer sense of this effect, try kneeling with a little sitting bench for support or sitting cross-legged on cushions directly on the ground, always with the hips a little higher than the knees. More of the body is in contact with the ground in both of these positions, and while they may feel a little awkward at first, there's a protective compactness to them that draws the body more fully into practice.

From whatever way of sitting or kneeling you can manage, shift your perspective on gravity from *It's weighing me down* to *It's holding me up*. From this perspective, gravity can have a distinctive quality of depth, if you pay attention to it. That quality is groundedness, arising from the stately mass of the planet beneath you, seating you home.

Energy

In addition to these interacting elements of the poise of musculature, the structure of bone, and the foundation of gravity, there's a fourth, energetic component involved in sustaining a sitting posture, which comes to the fore as the first three we've just visited are arranged and arrange themselves into that posture. Our bodies have no instantaneously steady state. They gestate, mature, flourish, decline, and die.

From moment to moment, they are in flux, they are happening, they are life's elaborations. That flux is life. Your body *is* your life.

As you sit there, you are respiring, metabolizing, strengthening, growing, weakening, ageing. You are continuously gestating the life you were given and the life you will engender. You are living your life, and you are dying your life. This fourth force incorporated in your posture is the force of life, the intense and visceral expression of your life, its arrow. As you find your way into a sitting posture and reconcile the physical forces involved, pay attention to the unimpedable mystery of this animating force, life's presence present, its energy coursing through your body, shining out as the body is stilled.

Spine

The essential feature of the classical posture, though, is the straight spine with the head in perfect alignment, the crown extended upward, resulting in the chin dropping slightly toward the chest. Where have you seen this gesture before, and what does it portend? Catch any animal unawares, and it will present you with a raised head on an extended neck. This is the instinctive choreography of alertness, everything else suspended in the moment as vigilance possesses the attention and the body. It is this gesture at the centre of the sitting posture that animates the whole undertaking and expresses its true intent.

In both concentration and insight practice, you will be bringing all of your attention to the object of concentration, poised like a soaring hawk, spying on your mind, primed for the slightest flicker of recognition. When you find your practice getting dull, bring it back to life by, smoothly and in sequence, planting your tail bone, tilting your pelvis slightly forward, relaxing the shoulders, dropped and back, raising and opening the chest, tucking the chin slightly, and elongating the neck. The flow of that sequence of motions will naturally extend from the base of your spine up through the crown of your head like a wave, rekindling the energy of vigilance. When you find your practice scattered and intractable, relax that extension slightly along its entire extent; stand down from your post for a moment to collect yourself before returning to it more gently. The posture is tall and compact. From here, you will see everything.

Posture

Assemble an initial posture that balances and enlivens these muscular, structural, gravitational, and vivifying forces in a supportable way. There is nothing useful or admirable in discomfort. Set up a posture as close as possible to one of the classical sitting or kneeling postures, but remember that your body will have its own particular capabilities and limits.[2]

Over time, as a result of practice and a natural settling, your body will find its own way to the closest approximation to one of the classical postures that works best for you. At the outset, if you need to adjust, adjust. Be pliant with the body while it too is learning.

Your body is the platform for practice, the bedrock. Your body is the way in which your being has touched down on this earth, and it's the way in which it will depart in the end. In the escalating sequence of practices that follow, we will become familiar with always unwinding back to the body as the ever-orienting support for sitting practice, always there.

Moreover, once we come to the insight practices, the body will serve as an exquisitely sensitive Geiger counter for even the most fleeting blips of the reactivity with which we will principally be occupied.

After you have been practising in a particular posture for some time, go back and re-examine the principles of the classical postures, and revisit your own with an eye to adjusting it into closer correspondence with one of them. You should arrive at a posture that not only works for you but begins to reward you with ease and pliancy. Once you have found this particular composition, regard it as perfect. What started out looking like just sitting there has turned out to be intuitively and exquisitely tuned. Your body is the perfect platform from which to encounter your being.

Interlude

The preceding has been a careful examination of the dynamics of the sitting posture, perhaps a bit obvious and belaboured, enough so that you may have read through it without putting it into practice. If so, you will have missed a valuable opportunity.

Examining your body and your posture to set up a posture for practice requires that you start noticing. If you found the examination overly subtle and elusive, be forewarned: this is a mild introduction to the even more persnickety detail we're going to delve into in the concentration practices, and the even more elusive detail we're going to delve into in the insight practices. You are starting to rehabilitate the surroundings in which you have been living your interior life, reclaiming and enlivening the original gifts you started out with but which have fallen into neglect. You are identifying the most stripped-away fundamentals from which experience arises. This examination of the dynamics of your body may come across as elementary, but it turns out you can come back to it again and again, long after you have seamlessly integrated your posture into your practice, and there it will be, something unnoticed, just waiting on your recognition.

One of the most beautiful notions at the centre of the traditions in which these practices originated is the idea that you already have everything you need, not just to practise, but to become free. Your entanglement is of your own making, and your own obliviousness is hiding from you your ability to free yourself. Skipping over this examination of your body and the posture because it strikes you as obvious and belaboured is the beginning of a cascade of dissipating evasions that sustains that oblivion.

While the outcome of these practices can be truly remarkable, anticipation of the remarkable might mislead you into expecting a magic wand with which to open the doors. There isn't one. Instead, it's these unassuming fundamentals of body, and eventually of mind, that will come together to liberate you. But first, you must find these fundamentals where they are hiding in plain sight—sight so plain that you dismiss it. So if you didn't follow along with this investigation of your body and posture, consider going back and doing so now, in the interest of the particular knowledge it will give you regarding your posture, and for the general practice it will give you in starting to notice.

Eyes

The classic instructions for the eyes are that they should be downcast and slightly open. There are good reasons for this.

First, open eyes keep you awake in the world and establish the sight of that world in your practice from the outset. While we will begin by emphasizing the abatement of vision in practice, we will ultimately bring it fully back into the equation, where it will serve an indispensable role in insight. If you have been concentrating with your eyes closed, the introduction of vision at that point will upend any composure you have managed to establish, and you'll be back at square one.

Second, lowering and raising the gaze can be used to tune the amount of light you are experiencing, and that amount of light is in lockstep with the energy of concentration. It's the light you are calibrating, not the content of the visual field. If you find yourself slow and sleepy, raise the gaze to add energy to your concentration. If you find yourself agitated and scattered, lower the gaze to calm things down. Try this now, noting the dynamics as you do, so that you are familiar with the effectiveness of this tool for when it occurs to you that you need it.

Breath

Throughout the calm-abiding concentration practices, the breath will be the exclusive object of concentration, at first intensely, as the central point around which to collect and calm your attention, but eventually easily, as the steady keel it is, and relative to which everything else is transitory. It has anchoring and guiding qualities that imbue your practice. And, as luck would have it, you are never without it.

The breath is of your essence as an animal. It trails you all the way back to the moment of your birth. There is nothing in your memory since that doesn't have the breath as a backdrop.

Above all, the breath as the object of concentration is inexhaustible. In practice, you will watch as it unfurls from its visceral roots into an entrancing sensual event, into a hovering beacon of pure occurrence, into a shimmering flow of the grains of sand of the mind itself, into durationless dust motes in the sunlight of awareness, into nothing but effervescence, until its own ground is all that's left. This display is not out there; it's in the nature of your breath. But I'm getting ahead of myself.

. . .

You are about to arrange your body into a balanced and sustainable but unfamiliar posture, keep your eyes open to the awake world, and practise bringing your restless attention exclusively to your breath. You will have to practise again and again, to fail, to persevere, and to find it all worth your while. When all of this seems least doable, give yourself over to the breath now and again, let it carry you and guide you on its own until you can get your oar back into the stream and take up your practice once again.

Imagination

In the midst of practising, in the midst of being assiduous and practical and eager and hopeful, you may occasionally come to a complete, black, implacable dead end. There is nothing like these undeserved but comprehensive frustrations for weighing your practice down with cynicism and doubt, some of which you may be inclined to project upon your teacher, or your fellow students who seem to be making undisturbed progress. At times such as these, you have at hand the most powerful tool of them all, your imagination.

There is no part of practice that is imaginary, no part of direct experience that is imaginary, no part of the consequences of either for your daily life that is imaginary. Imagination is a tool, not a destination, and, imaginatively deployed, it can be a source of incomparable inspiration for your practice. Indeed, there are times when nothing else will serve.

For instance, you may already have experimented with a grounded, stable, poised posture and experienced it as something less than grounded, stable, and poised. Rummage around in your imagination for some totem of composure drawn from your most accustomed sensual realm: a warm shaft of sunlight dropping through a window; a foghorn, deep and sonorous; a pale, wet stone nestled in the moss of the forest floor; the smell of rain; the rising moon; the opalescent surface of a lake at dawn. Let the self-composure of your chosen image deepen and radiate in your imagination, and then let it soak into your body. Hold it there.

Now consider that all the stability and poise you are perceiving in that image is projected. Everything you attribute to it is natural to you, yours already. Release all the energy of the awkwardness, the restlessness, the self-consciousness you feel in your posture into the resolving presence of the image, so it becomes even more companionable. Become that exemplar yourself. Finally, and most importantly, let the image go, return to your practice, and see who it is that's sitting there now.

In the pages that follow, you will find traces of my own imaginative muses—sailing, in particular—which I do not hesitate to use to evocatively flesh out the experience of practice. As your practice develops, cultivate this remarkable power of your own imagination for invocation and transformation—not just for sweeping aside what appear to be insurmountable barriers, but also for enhancing the depth, momentum, even the variety of your practice.

Take whatever imaginative analogies I offer and transform them, and anything else you need, into personally resonant forms, forms that come from your own depths, that have some element of freedom-making, forms that express for you an image of both longing and liberation. These will become the imaginative forces that will catalyze shifts in your practice far more handily than brute endurance. Deploy this tool carefully and selectively, setting it aside once it has served its purpose, so that nothing but your own direct experience is speaking to you. You want always to be able to say, when accused of it, "Of course I'm imagining things."

Vigilance

You will use your body to set up a grounded, stable, poised posture, at first with a fair amount of attention and intent, but eventually effortlessly, even thoughtlessly. Your body will come to take care of itself. You will use your imagination contingently, bringing it into the service of your practice for specific purposes, and then setting it aside in favour of direct experience. But vigilance you will deploy continuously.

To be vigilant is to be "on the lookout." Vigilance is the preparedness to recognize. It is your sentinel. Concentration and insight practice each have their descriptions, their exercises, their commentaries, their devices and supports, and you will take up each of these in the process of practising. But your steady state will be one of vigilance, of a mind primed for recognition.

Vigilance may seem effortful at first, like bending spoons. That effortfulness can tire and discourage and frustrate you, but this is to be expected of withdrawal from the seductive fun of endless distraction. With practice and experience, however, you will find that vigilance is an expansive and resplendent state capable of sustaining itself. That might not sound convincing, but an exploration of vigilance in action might persuade you that it is a faculty if not of ease, then at least of a more subtle character than you credit it.

Imagine you're in an airport, looking for the friend you've come to meet amongst a stream of people disembarking from a flight. This is a binary task: as each person emerges, you do or do not recognize them as the friend you're looking for. If you do, the vigilance you brought to the task evaporates, replaced by social engagement with your friend. If you don't, that person disappears, replaced by the next candidate in the stream. This is a sort of keyhole vigilance, arriving at the familiar with satisfaction.

Now imagine you've arrived late. Your friend has already disembarked and is somewhere in the crowd in the arrivals hall. This is a sweeping kind of vigilance, sweeping over the whole crowd again and again, everyone a candidate on every sweep, since you aren't remembering the non-matching faces you've already swept over. But it's also definitive vigilance in the sense that the task has a single, known, successful outcome, arriving at the familiar with relief.

Now imagine you've come to the airport to catch a flight yourself. It doesn't depart for another couple of hours, so you while away your time observing the crowd in the departure hall, wondering if there's anyone you might recognize. This is diffuse vigilance. Both the crowd and your gallery of acquaintances are various, so you must be open to a match occurring without any direction on your part, other than being vigilant. If a match occurs, you arrive at the familiar with surprise.

Finally, imagine you hear someone in the departure lounge, sitting a few seats away from you, suddenly say, with a shadow of tension in their voice, "What's going on over there?" and you follow their gaze. Suspense will bring energy, even vividness to your vigilance, and yet you have no idea what you're looking for. For a few seconds, everything in the world apart from your present situation vanishes. You may even feel a bit disembodied as your attention flares up like a laser against an undifferentiated backdrop of sheer potential, a potential that could possibly resolve in alarm. All by itself, vigilance has commandeered the proceedings to its own ends, shining and exclusive, almost ruthless.

Imagine being able to bring this full range of the scope, brightness, elasticity, and incisiveness of vigilance to an encounter with the nature of your mind.

Direct experience

The final tool you have at your disposal is recognition in the incontestable field of your own direct experience—experience before anything has been made of it—recognition as a non-conceptual capacity of mind. The phrase "field of your own direct experience" conveys the key principle that recognition in this context is not something you do, it's something that occurs on its own.

The field of direct experience will not just serve as the ground from which recognition will arise. It will also determine the shape and character of how your practice will unfold. The sequence of practices that follows is presented according to an ancient pedagogy structured more in the interests of preserving the instructions than in mirroring any one person's experience. Your own trajectory will be determined by what arises in your direct experience as a result of practising according to the pedagogy. The process is one of catalysis rather than prescription.

Recognition not only reveals and confirms an immediate experience; it also functions like echolocation, leaving you to discern the contours of the underlying landscape from which experience is arising. This is why only you can navigate your path through these practices. You must be open to everything your teachers and the traditions are trying to tell you, at the same time never wavering from the beacon of direct experience. It can be a rough-and-tumble process of figuring out to whom and to what to listen, when, and how.

All of practice will be directed toward setting up the conditions for recognition to occur, so all your doing will be circumstantial, like drawing a wild animal out into the open by not making eye contact with it. You will have to be earnest in your practice to become as unsuspecting as possible for the nature of your mind to start to flicker into view.

Day-to-day experience, for all its apparent fluidity, is a rigidified precipitate out of the original undifferentiated flux of the mind. Even with the most elementary of the calm-abiding concentration practices, the experiences that will consolidate these practices for you occur just ahead of rigidifying conceptualization. You must learn to cultivate recognition outside of the context of thinking, and you'll get practice with this from the outset. Your capacity for recognition does not need to be learned anew—it's already there. The focus of practice is getting out of recognition's way.

Practise

For a few minutes, try out whatever posture you've come up with. Assemble the arrangement of limbs that works for you, checking in particular for a straight, slightly extended spine. Let your eyes settle into an unfocused, downcast gaze that withdraws you from the world without making you drowsy. Then gently behold the breathing body, the breath in the body.

Take an expansive but alert stance. After a few minutes, adjust your posture first to relax and then to re-extend the spine, and note any effects that result, be they physical or emotional or in the state of your mind. Raise and then lower the gaze a little, noting whether you can detect an energetic shift in either the body or the mind as you do.

Find a neutral, stable arrangement of your spine and your gaze, settle into your posture once again, and try not so much to concentrate as to give yourself over to the life in your body as it manifests in the breath. Simultaneously, follow the beat of your heart right into your heart, and practise from there.

What is it about this experience that feels unfamiliar, and what is it that feels deeply familiar?

At the outset, practice will consist of sitting on a chair or on a cushion on the floor, or of kneeling on a bench in a posture of sustained stimulation and effortlessness. Your sole task will be to bring your attention to your breath and keep it there. To do so, you will apply skills you will learn, and deploy capacities native to your mind, to develop and expand your experience with concentration as you go. At the end of each sit, however brief or extended, disruptive or revealing, don't just get up and walk away. As you return to your ordinary state of mind, take a few moments to review your practice so as to consolidate and extend your skill with concentration. Remark upon and appreciate both what you found corroborating and what you found challenging. Then do all this all over again and again and again.

Eventually, reverberations of your on-the-cushion experience will follow you off the cushion by way of greater self-awareness of distraction and reactivity. With time, some of that experience will show up as gentle moderation of both of these afflictions, the first flickers of liberation softening the edges of your lived life. Practice will become much more than this as your experience with both concentration and insight progresses, until there is seldom a moment in your life when you aren't aware of the journey you are undertaking here.

Fare well

You started out this exploration of the tools for practice innate to the standard-issue human being with the simple exercise of standing with your feet together and closing your eyes. But that small, opening endeavour bears the hallmarks of the entire path of practice. You used your body to discover a posture of stability, ease, and poise upon which to base a sitting practice. Then you considered detail with the eyes, the breath, imagination, vigilance, and direct experience. But something more fundamental has just taken place.

For starters, you showed up. Here you are, reading this book, paying some attention to what it has to say. Whatever your reservations, for now you opened up a bit, you chose to consider its ideas. You even gave some of them a try. And even if it was only reluctantly, you looked directly at the experience of your life in your body, you put your ear to its ground. You involved yourself in minute particulars in the roaring sea of everything else. Perhaps you recognized subtle distinctions in that experience. You might not use the same words to describe them as were used to bring them to your attention, but you know those distinctions in your own way now. You changed. All of practice unfolds like this. Already the thing has touched you.

PART II

CALM ABIDING

3

CAPACITIES

The calm-abiding concentration practices were cast into a pedagogy known as the Nine Stages of Sustained Attention centuries ago, and these ancient instructions are full of detail and precision.[1] The traditional sources on the topic are aimed more at teachers than at students. The accompanying iconography, known as The Elephant Path, is a cautionary tale about the twists and turns, perils and pitfalls on the path to calm abiding, with little to say about how to actually practise.[2] The traditional instructions emphasize states of mind at each stage, the impediments to and flaws in those states, and the correctives for them.[3] I have always found it a trap to be looking for any particular state in practice; besides, as a practitioner, I find descriptions of states unconvincing, and as a Canadian, I find them embarrassing. States are not inconsequential, it's just that every description of them is subjective, relevant only to the specific practitioner.

Instead of states and the flaws in them, I emphasize the capacities of mind that I find to be characteristic of each stage. There are direct correlates for these nine capacities in the traditional descriptions of the stages, where they are presented as achievements resulting from corresponding "powers."[4] Those powers are necessary to the practice, but in my experience, they don't result in the capacities so much as they uncover and enable them. Acquiring new abilities is a very different task from discovering those you already have. All of practice takes place in the presence of an extant potential and instinct for liberation, awaiting recognition in your direct experience.

With each of these nine capacities of mind, your task is to identify the capacity itself, that is, to recognize what your mind is naturally capable of doing, and then to deploy it—use your attention and intention to bring that capacity to bear upon practice. You can then focus on getting the practice right and let the state be what it may. Take each capacity and turn it from an idea explained here on paper into an experience that you are able to describe for yourself and to your teacher.

Simultaneously with practice, you want to start to notice the quality of concentration that results when practice starts to come together. Recognition functions to reacquaint you with the qualities of mind you will begin to uncover. When these qualities show up, however vaguely and tentatively as your experience with each practice evolves, occasionally give yourself over to the contemplative perception of the state of your mind. Let it become familiar, sink in, but without loss of concentration. Combine the intent of the instructions with the actual experience that turns up in practice. They are, by definition, a perfect match.

Teachers and teachings

In what follows, I will be describing in my own way the progression of concentration practices as they were taught to me. By doing so, I hope not only to inspire you to undertake these practices, but also to give you an idea of what you can expect any teacher to teach you. An experienced teacher should be able to recognize particular states from your description of your state of mind in your own words. In identifying these states back to you, the teacher fosters the integration of your practice, but only to the extent that you are willing and able to recognize and respond to the voice of experience in what you are being taught. The traditions emphasize the human lineage of these teachings: for their maximum effectiveness, they rely on the indelibly human interaction between someone who has been there and someone who is just finding their way.

In choosing a teacher, you want to have some confidence that they speak from experience, not just with their own practice but also with the traditional teachings on the nine-stages pedagogy.[5] While they are not well known or commonly taught in the West, the original texts on the topic of calm-abiding concentration practice are more than a thousand years old, so there's been lots of time for everyone to catch up.

Keep in mind that the arrangement of these teachings into nine stages is for pedagogical purposes. Each practitioner's path through them will be squiggly and erratic. However quickly either the instructions or your fellow practitioners seem to be progressing, work with a personally doable practice that both strengthens your newly built basis and challenges you to extend it.

Should you consult them for yourself, the traditional sources describing these practices can come across as mannered and formulaic. Read them with discernment, and put them into practice with improvisation, translating and transforming them to craft practices that work for you in this very different world of ours. Tradition is a cypher; authentic practice is the outcome of decoding it on your own terms.

Pliancy

Underlying the nine stages, with their states, powers, flaws, and antidotes, are the practice skills required to embark on and traverse the path through those stages. The next three chapters detail six such skills, and into the description of those skills I have woven the description of the nine capacities of mind I found to be characteristic of the corresponding nine stages the skills are intended to take you through.[6]

These skills are everything you need to establish, build, and enrich a concentration practice, and to make your way through all of the stages. As with any learning, there will be some awkwardness with these skills before there is ease, but it will come. To get beyond ease to pliancy, you want to learn to play with each skill to calibrate its dynamic range, and to notice the effects on your practice within that range.[7]

By "pliancy" I mean resilient flexibility in general. Pliancy supports durability by allowing you to adapt your practice to the circumstances of the moment—your level of energy, or comfort, or distraction, or motivation, and so on—and it supports gracefulness by allowing you to transition your practice as those circumstances change.

For instance, one day you may find that a morning mist has come in, and there's not a sound in the city. The diffuse light brings a sense of calm and detachment, and your morning exercise has left your body limber and at ease. You set up your posture precisely, you distance yourself from sensory input in any form, and with the slightest inflection, you establish close and unwavering absorption with the intricacies of the breath. Then, as the session unfolds, you notice a sense of tightness has snuck up on you, so you drop into your body a little more loosely, open to the silence a little more expansively, and give the breath over to itself a little more. You have made a transition from closely held intent to more ease, and you continue your practice from there.

Another day, you may find that the racket of the city is grinding, some bill you owe is overdue, and too sudden a movement while lifting a box of books yesterday has left you oddly stooped. You set up your posture gingerly and with whatever latitude you need to avoid discomfort. You direct your attention gently to the felt sense of the body, as a refuge against the noise, and you establish a companionable following of the broadest outlines of the breath. Then, as the session unfolds and you collect yourself, you straighten your spine a bit, extricate yourself from the soundscape, and move in closer and more intimately with the breath. You have made a transition from loosely held intent to more liveliness, and you continue your practice from there.

Pliancy brings richness to practice. Initially within the range of each skill, but eventually within the range of the qualities of concentration that arise, you can find subtler and subtler variety. One day, you can return to one of the most basic practices you have learned and find that it offers up some new facet or nuance you are sure you have yet to experience. Or you can be practising at the leading edge of your path, attending carefully in a particular direction, when something quite other, replete and complete, slides in underneath everything and supplants it.

Even more beautifully, within insight practice, pliancy gives you not just the ability to tune your practice to a point of gyroscopic stability and self-sustainment; it also gives you the resilience you will need to accommodate the reverberations of insight when it dawns. While much of insight unfolds by diffusion, the way a morning mist lifts to reveal the day, it can also emerge suddenly, with excitement and emotion. When it does, you want to be flexible enough to fully experience these side effects but eventually release them, relying instead on the depths they leave in their wake.

As you progress through the skills and the stages, pause frequently to consolidate your practice by exploring and expanding the dynamic range of the skills you are learning, and whatever qualities arise in your practice. In this way, you will become a supple as well as an adept practitioner.

Practice

At the outset, your practice will revolve around your time spent sitting on the cushion, but you may notice that it starts to seep into your life off the cushion, unbidden. Initially, this self-propagation may be negative: you become aware of how scattered you can get, whereas before, you were just scattered, which is more peaceful than knowing you are. Or it occurs to you, with a twinge of guilt and a countermanding nodding off into rationalization, that you have not kept up your practice, you've given up on it, and you want to forget it. But it seems not to have forgotten you, irritating you when you're off the cushion.

Eventually, when you find a practical, sustainable, and sufficiently rewarding habit of practice in your life, your off-the-cushion practice will start to manifest as spontaneous integration of the positive qualities—mostly imperturbability—of your on-the-cushion experience, right there in broad daylight in your daily life. Irritation or integration, you can acknowledge them both as the harbingers of your freedom.

I wrote in the introduction that the fundamental freedom at stake here is the freedom to live as who you truly are by coming to terms with your own unmediated reactivity. I described this as a journey of liberation in which concentration practice is intended to gain freedom for yourself, and insight practice to gain freedom from yourself.

For me, liberation is not some moment toward which I am practising, it's the process of practice itself. Liberation is *becoming* free. It is a way of living that is not simply looking forward to ultimate equanimity and compassion; it is a way of living that constantly lives and nurtures everyday equanimity and compassion in every moment.

Starting here with the calm-abiding concentration practices, simply attending to your breath, may seem an unpromising way to set out on this quest for freedom, yet it will turn out to be quite the challenge in itself. It's a profound gesture of self-respect to create a space in your life for your mind to come forth untrammelled, to create the conditions for a blunt but compassionate appraisal of your predicament.

With the subsidence of distraction and the flourishing of equipoise will come the beginning of relief from the entanglement of reactivity. Not sustained relief, at the outset, but enough to let you know you are onto something. You will be placing your being back in your body and coming to your senses. You will be reclaiming your dignity. Setting out on this quest to come to terms with your reactivity, however tentatively and hopefully, is—every step of the way, no matter how small—nothing less than a wholehearted commitment to your own liberty.

EACH OF THE concentration and insight practices will be introduced with an intuitive description that should be intelligible to all readers. As each practice is expanded upon, though, it may become less easy to understand or to relate to, let alone to practise. Depending on your own inclination to and experience with the contemplation of your mind, you may find yourself with some degree of understanding and some degree of perplexity. Don't let the latter delay you.

Glean what orientation, perhaps even inspiration, you can from the descriptions so that you have a general idea of the progress of the practices, and then move through them with whatever facility comes to you. In time, your developing experience with concentration and insight will acquaint you with the full richness of all of these practices.

4

PLACING AND STAYING

Placing

To set out on your journey through the nine stages, the first practice to learn is the practice of just placing your mind on the object of concentration. I say "just" not to indicate that the task is simple, but to indicate this is all you will be doing, although it will turn out to be quite enough for now.

From your posture of stability and alertness, eyes downcast and partially open, spine straight and supple, attend to your breath, to the whole physical sensation of the breath in your body. For this practice, I was taught to attend to the felt sense of the in-breath, followed by the felt sense of the out-breath, followed by the felt sense of the whole body in whatever interval occurs between the breaths.

The felt sense of the whole body can feel like a different object of concentration from the breath. While this discontinuity can foster pliancy with the object of concentration, it can also have the effect of weakening the association of the breath with the body, risking the detachment of the object of concentration from the body.

In whatever interval occurs between the end of the out-breath and the beginning of the in-breath, I found it helpful to attend instead to the felt sense of *the breath in* the body, regarding the body as still in a breathing state.

The result is a three-phase object of concentration, all three phases of which are states of breathing, and all three phases of which are in the body: the felt sense of the in-breath, followed by the felt sense of the out-breath, followed by the felt sense of the breath in the body in whatever interval occurs between the breaths. With this three-phase object, practise directly with what's going on in the physical body. Try that for a few minutes, and note how much time you spend during the session absorbed exclusively with the three phases of the breath, the object of concentration.

THIS FIRST PRACTICE is likened to tuning into a particular frequency on a radio, but a better comparison would be tuning into a particular frequency on a radio in a room full of other radios, independently scanning from frequency to frequency. Each of your senses is jittering away with its own compelling news: *Look at that! What do I hear? My back aches!* Your thoughts see it as their duty never to stop, and your attempts to ignore them will be met with even more rebellious behaviour. Your imagination will try to rescue you from all this with its usual creativity and seductiveness. Your emotions will follow in train.

If you are like most human beings in the modern world, your first attempts at this practice will yield but a few seconds of absorption here and there before you find yourself derailed by distraction once again. Any sense you have of staying with the object of concentration is likely a side effect of multitasking, being clever about being distracted. Whatever the nature of your mind was when you were born, it has been obscured by a persistent racket. You may be struck by the extent of the losses you have sustained and of your own involvement in perpetuating them.

These first steps of practice are easily the most difficult and, in a way, the saddest. But they are also a remarkable victory. Even a sit full of distraction is a sit during which you are at least aware of how distracted you are. You have won the awareness of your reactivity, uncomfortable as that may be. Return to practice trusting that all the capacities you require to pick out and attend to the object of concentration are already native to your mind. Trust that when you have them in hand, you will be able to develop the kind of poised, stable concentration required for the insight practices. Calm-abiding concentration practice is the practice of sheltering the mind from further wear and tear so that these capacities can come forth on their own.

THE FIRST CAPACITY of mind to bring to bear is the capacity to pick out the object of concentration from the background of self-talk and thought. This capacity is the mind's native ability first to differentiate the noise of experience into signals, and then to bring one signal into the foreground from all the rest. The accompanying skill is then to place your attention upon the object of concentration, but you would have no candidate if the mind didn't distinguish one for you.

Practise again for a few minutes, recognizing that this ability to recover from distraction by picking out the object of concentration is native to the mind, never not at hand. Yes, mostly it's a mess, but every now and then, you recognize that and you re-place your attention on the object of concentration. In this moment, attend to this breath here and now, and then this breath here and now, and then again and again. Renew the practice in each instant, so that what happened in the last instant and what will happen in the next are forgotten, each instant independent in time. You may have a sense of self-talk and thought flaring up during this exercise, but that's just a result of a change in perspective, not an increase in activity. All that activity has been there all along; you are just used to the buzz.

This first practice is recognizing that you've lost the object of concentration, and the first capacity of mind is the ability to pick that object out again, creating the opportunity for you to place your attention back on it. Practise picking it out again and again so that your sense of this ability as a specific and almost autonomous agent is right there at your disposal. You only stop picking out the object of concentration when it stops falling out of your mind.

We take this capacity for granted, failing to realize that without it operating pretty much continuously and automatically, we would experience a barrage of perceptions and be helpless, in the face of their flow, to select anything in particular. The exercise is as much learning to pick out the object of concentration when it goes missing as it is coming to realize that you have the perfect tool for this practice.

Any sense that you are helpless in the face of the cacophony of your mind is misplaced. This capacity is one of the mind's most basic capabilities, one with which we can begin to differentiate and order experience. For such a tiny gesture, it's a workhorse.

Try again. You are attending to the unfolding physical events: the felt sense of the in-breath, followed by the felt sense of the out-breath, followed by the felt sense of the breath in the body in whatever interval occurs between the breaths. Calm-abiding concentration is more elemental than a thought process or a mental activity; it's more like finding a bearing on a compass.

. . .

Placing and Staying

WHEN YOU MANAGE to engage the object of concentration, take a moment to discern whether what you are attending to is the experience of the breath in your physical body, or whether you are attending instead to a rendering of it either in imagination (an image or animation of the breath) or in thought (the idea of the breath) or some other sly facsimile. Catch these distinctions early, since if you miss them, your practice will neither stabilize nor deepen. Both an image and a concept of the breath will have a disembodied aspect. Images tend to lead to torpor and dreaming, concepts tend to lead to agitation and boredom.

Try again. Experiment with these distinctions to reinforce your ability to detect that you are attending to the felt sense of the breath in the body rather than to either of these renderings. Take up the physical sensation of the breath in your body, the kinaesthetic sense of breathing. Then, let your engagement with the object of concentration slacken into something of an overlaid image of the breath as a current or mist, or as the sound of the wind in the trees. Switch back and forth between the kinaesthetic sense and the overlaid image until you have a distinctive sense of the dreaminess of the imaginative rendering.

Then, once again with the kinaesthetic sense of breathing as the object of concentration, let it drift into some idea about the breath, the words "the breath," or your knowledge of your breath or the activity of breathing. Switch back and forth between the kinaesthetic sense and the idea of the breath until you have a distinctive sense of the disembodiment of the conceptual rendering.

This active variation of the experience of the breath while you are practising is an instance of pliancy with the object of concentration, an exercise that makes settling on the proper object more stable and assured.

Protect

What I've laid out here may not seem like an imposing task, nor promise much in the way of usefulness, and yet it can be the occasion for a disproportionate amount of distraction. Both the precariousness of the exercise and the difficulty of putting it into practice offer rich and irresistible opportunities to give up the endeavour as misguided and unpromising.

To guard against these discouragements, take a moment after every sit, not just to review your experience but to protect your practice from falling apart due to disappointment or fatigue or neglect. This is an essential step, one specifically intended to create certainty and confidence in your practice.[1] It's you deciding to take responsibility for and care of both yourself and your practice, acknowledging that you are the sole custodian and champion of both.

You may be focussed on what practice promises, so much so that you aren't acknowledging what it is yielding. As hopeful for the future as you may be, take the time to acknowledge what your practice is revealing to you here and now, in the present. Some days, that may be something new and moving and profound; other days, it may just be one more occasion for not giving up. In either case, protecting serves to integrate and stabilize your practice each step of your way. Beginning here and throughout the remainder of the book, we'll pause occasionally to review, corroborate, and cherish the progress of the path in this way.

So CONSIDER what it is you are on the verge of learning at this point, what this racket is teaching you.

First is the proposition that there is a faculty of mind called attention, that attention can be directed by you to the object of concentration, that it can be detected to have wandered, and that it can be redirected back to the object of concentration. The distraction of attention creates the opportunity to recognize that it has wandered, and the opportunity to depend on a native capacity of the mind to pick out the object of concentration once again, enabling you to return your attention to it. It is as rich a lesson to recognize that your attention has been dislodged from the object of concentration as it is to recognize that your attention has remained engaged with it. If every failure is such an opportunity, you're in luck. You have so much to work with.

Second, the flavour of distraction you experience most persistently and most strongly is revealing to you the contours of your own constitution. Your distractions will come on the channel that is most natural to you; they will carry the signature of the particular individual you are. Some of us will find ourselves dithered by imagination, some tangled in thought, some churned by emotion, others impaled on physicality. Whatever frailties turn out to suit you, don't take them personally. It will turn out that they can eventually just be left on the shelf.

Third, the exquisite precision of delineating sensation from imagination, and both of these from thought, acquaints you with the agility of your attention and gives you the opportunity to play around with what you're supposed to be doing, as a way of reinforcing doing what you're supposed to be doing. While my technical training may have made learning these practices more of a struggle for me than for less encumbered students, it also gave me at least two helpful skills: an eye for subtle differences such as these, and an appreciation for the disproportionate consequences such differences can have.

Many of the lessons I learned along the way have this character: what you come to discern in your encounter with the mind may not amount to more than shaded inflections, but picking them out of the background not only throws them into relief—it fundamentally unstitches some enclosing context that had always seemed to be all of a piece.

At the centre of skill with these practices is the ability to recognize the state of your mind, and the ability to set up the conditions that will bring it into ever more complete and easeful absorption with the object of concentration. At this stage, it may seem as though you are doing both of these with thought, but in time and with practice, the character of these abilities will shift so that they are less thought-based and more automatic. This is the beginning of the emergence of a facility you have always possessed but have not often been pressed to use: the ability to be aware of the state of your mind, also known as metacognitive awareness.[2] Both recognition and intent will begin to arise from metacognitive awareness alone, and their sensitivity and effectiveness will increase with every minute of practice as they become exceedingly fine tools.

Staying

The second practice, once you are confident that you can always pick out the object of concentration from any state of distraction, is to keep your attention from falling off the object in the first place, to direct your attention to stay with it, to hold your attention on it.[3] "Keep," "direct," "hold"—these are all effortful words, and if you have some notion of concentration being an effort, it's probably these face-scrunching tasks you have in mind. It's true you'll have to do some work to make a start with concentration practice, but don't anticipate that continuous staying will be the result of some heroic capacity for endurance. No one could sit for long if it were.

From your posture of stability and alertness, eyes downcast and partially open, spine straight and supple, attend to your breath, to the felt sense of the breath in your body. Pick out the object of concentration, place your attention on it, and then just maintain the intention to stay with it. The intention to stay can be sustained even as the staying wobbles. The mind starts to stray, but you have a sense of that straying occurring in parallel with the intention not to stray.

Even distraction can be accompanied by an ongoing intention to stay, tinged with a little frustration. You watch distraction at work even as you make your way back to staying. Practise staying with the object without it dropping away from the centre of your attention. Practise like this until staying starts to take place on its own. Not for long at first, but long enough for you to experience a shift from effort to something more akin to coasting.

In the previous section on placing, the practice involved a fair amount of effort on your part: attending, redirecting, trying, failing, trying again. With this practice of staying, bring the same kind of effort and repetition to the practice to pick out and place your attention on the breath. But also approach it a bit like catching a wave. You need to do all the work to place yourself just so and to participate in the balance and attention that staying requires, but there will now be an aspect of the breath that carries you by itself.

Return to your posture of stability and alertness, eyes downcast and partially open, spine straight and supple, and attend to your breath, to the felt sense of the breath in your body, the felt sense of the in-breath, followed by the felt sense of the out-breath, followed by the felt sense of the breath in the body in whatever interval occurs between the breaths. When the object of concentration is steady and clear, try leaning into it, giving yourself over to its carrying capacity with the slightest shift of weight. Do this delicately at first, like pretending you can walk on water. With familiarity and trust, you will be able to depend more and more on the active buoyancy of the breath itself.

Practise frequently and for not too long, until some interval of staying is detectable in your own direct experience. "Frequently," "not too long," and "some interval" are yours to tune to your own temperament and abilities. Decide metrics based on your own understanding of practice, security of experience, and growing familiarity with recognition.

Accompanying your first experiences of staying may be an even brighter degree of disruption bound up in your distractions. In concentration practice, you are learning to let go of all the reactivity you have been rewarded for, underneath which you may find a fair degree of restlessness. But all that reactivity conceals a tremendous source of energy. Think of the relief you experience when some irritation that's gotten on your nerves—some itch, some flashing light, some buzz—subsides, and your sinews loosen, releasing the tension that had been clutching at the irritation even as you wanted to be rid of it.

Irritation leaves in its wake the energy you have invested in it. If you can let distractions unfold and expire, you can repurpose every one of them into a lift of energy for staying. When you find yourself in some flare-up of distraction, disarm it by regarding it not as an affliction but simply as a misplacement of energy, so that not only do you return to and stay with the object of concentration, you do so buoyed along by the radiance of the abandoned distraction.

STAYING IS A CONTINUITY OF AWARENESS, being present to the object of concentration. The first time you experience a few moments together of staying, you might be inclined to regard this as something that happened as a result of all your efforts. In the maelstrom of potential distractions available to you, how could something completely counter to that ruckus possibly become established? Certainly not by mere effort.

That continuity you experience is enabled by another capacity of mind in action, the capacity of the mind itself to maintain attention on the object of concentration across time, to stay with the object of concentration. I am distinguishing the staying you do, which is the practice, from the staying that then happens, which is the mind's native capacity taking over. Each time a few moments of staying on the object of concentration come together, your mind is showing you its familiarity with staying. It's showing you that in the presence of less noise, its natural condition is to abide calmly. And it's letting you know that you can start to trust it to be there for you.

Your first taste of staying might remind you of other instances in your experience of effortless mental absorption that caused everything else, including perhaps a sense of time, to fall away. You are not there yet with this particular practice, but you've caught a glimpse of a tremendous ability native to your mind. And you've had something of an easeful encounter with concentration, which can be confusing for those of us who excel at trying.

I wrote that one of the notable merits of the breath as the object of concentration is that it bears the imprint of the first recollection; it has a primordial place in the original constellation of your memory. Other than the beat of your heart, what other companion have you had since birth than the breath?

Can you find a way of remaining alert and attentive at the same time as you surrender? Relying on the practice experience to have its own energy and impetus is to begin to understand a guiding principle of both concentration and insight practice, a principle at the root of the central role recognition will have throughout your practice: not only do you already have all the tools you need for your quest, but you already know where you're going. You've just been hijacked along the way. Let yourself be persuaded of the opposite of an effortful approach. Be open to the warm current of return.

Not-seeing

To dispel any complacency that may accompany your new-found proficiency with staying, it's important to become aware of increasingly subtle gradations of staying. You can experience the subtlety of these gradations with the sense of sight. For this discussion, we'll consider three types of sight, each less elaborated. *Looking* is attentionally selecting something out of the visual field. *Seeing* is just being diffusely aware of the sense of sight in general. *Not-seeing* is releasing even this sense of sight until it drops out of awareness. Looking focuses on something specific in the visual field, seeing focuses on what we call the diffuse middle distance, and not-seeing has no focus.

In the instructions on posture, you were taught to keep the eyes partially open, the gaze downcast. Vision is such a dominant sense in most of us that in your first attempts at practice, though the domination of sight may have slackened as you attended to your breath, your gaze was still engaged in looking, insofar as you took any particular focus. Focus is the ability of the lens of the eye to pick something specific out of the visual field, as well as the almost unnoticed tendency of the mind to identify that something. They are usually, but not necessarily, coupled. Looking consists of attentionally selecting something out of the visual field in this way.

In terms of impediments to concentration, the mind's identification of the thing seen is the most important aspect of looking. Even as you may have a sense of continuous staying, if your eyes are looking at something with any sense of visual recognition—the floor in front of you, for instance—no matter how disengaged you may be in that looking, your attention is at best divided between the object of concentration and the looking at the floor. It's an easy distraction to catch, and the solution is to direct the downward gaze without focus, diffusely into the middle distance. Watch the attentional identification of "the floor" dissolve, and as you do, release the attention taken up by the looking so that it's free to be shifted to the object of concentration instead. Stay with this "seeing" as opposed to "looking" until you notice that you've drifted into "looking" again.

Work with this until it's natural for you to be able to recognize looking when it is happening, to relax the attention taken up by the looking by shifting your gaze to the middle distance, and to recognize the resulting enhancement of absorption with the object of concentration. Reinforce the recognition of this distinction further by switching back and forth between "looking" and "seeing" so that the different sense of them is clear to you.

There's a further refinement you can make. If you are now gazing without focus into the middle distance, you may be concentrating on the object of concentration, but that concentration will still be partial, depleted by the unfocused seeing that's going on, seeing still being evident as a visual field in awareness. The attention taken up with this seeing can be brought to bear on the object of concentration instead.

This shift from seeing to not-seeing is not as intuitive as the shift from looking to seeing, and there is no triggering physical prompt, such as a simple shift of focus. The practice is more like releasing. It involves some combination of relaxing attention to the visual field in favour of bringing greater attention to bear on the object of concentration. As you do that, the attention taken up by unfocused seeing can be drawn off the visual field and brought to bear instead on the object of concentration.

When this takes place, the visual field will still be present—your eyes are open, after all—but you will be unaware of it.

You will not be seeing it. You won't notice that you are not-seeing until seeing kicks in again. In fact, you can't notice not-seeing until seeing re-emerges. Not-seeing can only be detected in hindsight. In not-seeing, the distraction of the visual field has vanished even as the field itself remains present; you just don't see it. When seeing drops away like this, the quality of the concentration that results is quietly opulent and deeply familiar.

You have already experienced this shift. Think of a time when you got lost in thought and something occurred in front of you to snap you "back to reality." The visual field, which had dropped away due to neglect while still not going dark, suddenly flashed up before your eyes with the jolt to your attention. You weren't blind in the meantime; the visual field was still present, but it was consuming none of your attention. While your mind was elsewhere, you were not-seeing.

It doesn't make a lot of sense to talk about practising not doing something, like remembering to forget. It's more accurate to say that the not-doing will be the outcome of *setting up the conditions* for not-doing to occur by itself. And setting up the conditions is something you can practise. The conditions to set up for not-seeing are first, recognizing any seeing going on, and then, simultaneously releasing that seeing and shifting the weight of your attention more fully to the object of concentration. While you can't directly detect the shift to not-seeing, you can become familiar with the pooling depth of concentration that results. This indirect, hands-off approach to setting up conditions is characteristic of the insight practices, so start to develop some facility with it here.

A similar exercise can be done with both hearing and physical sensation. The utility of dropping sensory input completely while the senses themselves are still very much alive lies in deepening your engagement with the object of concentration, not in achieving a state of sensory deprivation.

There's a longer-term outcome as well, and it applies when the senses are allowed once again to run their course—which, it will turn out, we will need them to be doing. When you open back up to the panoply of all your senses, which you'll do at different times in both concentration and insight practice, the coercive way in which they are representing an objective world to you will show up more evidently as the creative way in which they are making that world up. They will be revealed to be the animators they are. You will catch them making up what you believe. You can hold them in more playful regard.

Taking whichever of the senses is most intuitive for you, spend some time with this exercise, moving your attention from the selective perceiving to the diffuse perceiving and then to the released not-perceiving mode, stopping for a while in each to become familiar with the attendant quality of staying.

A SIDE EFFECT of the resulting more complete staying is that a third capacity of mind comes into play. As a result of your heightened sensitivity to the quality of staying, you will come to recognize distraction more swiftly, closer to its onset. The contrast between staying and distraction will be heightened by the increased depth and engagement of staying, and that contrast makes the onset of distraction that much more unmissable.

Unlike the more stationary vigilance you have been deploying so far, this is an instance of active vigilance. It's the difference between saying, *Oh, there you are,* and saying, *Oh no you don't!* when recognizing distraction. In the former case, distraction is under way; in the latter, you catch it right at the moment it begins to wiggle and before it carries you away. It's not that you've suddenly become remarkably incisive, it's that this agile capacity of the mind is emerging on its own into the open air created by staying.

This correlation between depth of staying and speed of recognizing distraction is a display of the mind's own propensity for staying. What starts out as a task of achieving some kind of unfamiliar mental composure turns out to be something for which the mind has a knack. Rest assured that the ability to concentrate comes naturally to everyone. All of practice is constructive, and the pedagogy you have taken up is timeless and proven. Start trusting that you are finding your way to a place where you belong. Not only do you have the breath beckoning you home, you now have your mind longing to be there.

A NEGATIVE CONSEQUENCE of paying this kind of attention to your mind—and of vigilance in general—is that you may recognize certain recurring distractions that seem purpose-built to undermine your practice, as if they have hardly any other aim. Should frustration, discouragement, or any other disturbing emotion, even anger, be unsettling your concentration, regard it as a rebellion of the reactive mind itself, resentful of being displaced from its usual domination; it's fighting back. You are suffering from a self-attack.

Try not to accuse yourself of inadequacy. Instead, find a gentle, inspiring self-invocation with which to extricate yourself from the snare. Tend to yourself with compassion and kindness, since you are very much in your own care here. Know that the energy that will come from releasing the assault on yourself and whatever else you're flailing at can bring an attendant surge in the energy of your practice. Know that vigilance is at the root of recovery from victimization, and it is everything you need never to be at the mercy of your own mind again.

Protect

The concentration practices presented so far have been exploring the degree to which you have been attending to or distracted from the object of concentration, the degree to which the object of concentration was the felt sense of the breath in the body or some facsimile in imagination or thought, and the degree to which you have been attending completely or only partially to the object of concentration. This facility with exploring and then handling the dynamic range of practice—placement upon, identification of, and involvement with the object of concentration—is the pliancy of staying. It enables you to home in on the object of concentration, and it gives you the elasticity to stay with the object of concentration with poise and skill, eventually with ease. Much of the effort you bring to practice is to develop this ease.

You've been presented with a great deal to work with as you learn to place your attention soundly and assuredly on the object of concentration, and to stay with it in a delicate balance of effort and yielding. As a rough rule of thumb, if you are practising outside of retreat, give yourself at least a month or two of practising twice a day for at least ten to fifteen minutes to explore all the territory we've covered so far.

The most important aspect of your practice is that you deepen your familiarity with recognition—recognition of distraction, recognition of the quality of staying, recognition of the rendering of the object of concentration, recognition of the native capacities of mind—with recognition as an autonomous and self-reinforcing response of the mind. The central dynamic of sitting practice is reinforcement. At the end of every sit, take a few minutes to affirm all you have made of the time, and be careful with it.

From here on, proceed gingerly, as though you were recovering from brain damage.

The most important thing to do now is to keep your practice rich enough that recognition can continue to show up and display its calm knowing, so you come to trust it as the unerring guide to everything that lies ahead. Once you feel you're handy with pliantly directing and placing your attention on the object of concentration, and staying with it so that you have a few minutes at a time with the felt sense of the breath in the body completely, solely, and stably occupying your attention, step back for a moment and acknowledge just what it is you have regained.

You now have in hand the ability to clear and protect a natural space for yourself in the midst of the mayhem of your usual careening sense of experience, even if it's for just a few minutes. You can create an imperturbable grove in the midst of your life in which simply to be. This space indelibly stakes out your claim to your own liberty. It is the home and reservoir of all the patience and commitment you have shown in coming this far, and which you will need for everything that is to come. It's your declaration that you will no longer be lulled along in life by the tethers of reactivity. Above all, you have found a way to spend some time caring for and in the care of your mind in its natural, open state. You can begin to get to know yourself at last.

5
REFINING AND INTENSIFYING

Refining

Once you are able pliantly to direct and place your attention on the breath in the body, and stay absorbed with it for a few minutes at a time, you can enhance the stability, durability, and resilience of your practice by attending more closely to the detail in the object of concentration. Refining that detail gives you the opportunity to develop two further capacities of mind: the capacity for recognizing the quality of your concentration, and the capacity for savouring that quality, for the mind to be drawn into practice by that quality.

For this practice, I was taught to refine the three-phase object of concentration into seven phases. Attend to the first movement of the in-breath, then to the full duration of the in-breath, and then to the last movement of the in-breath. Then attend to the first movement of the out-breath, then to the full duration of the out-breath, and then to the last movement of the out-breath. In whatever interval occurs between the end of exhalation and the beginning of inhalation—between the breaths—attend to the felt sense of the breath in the body.

At the outset, distinguishing these separate phases can feel awkward and disruptive, especially since you have taken such care to develop a few minutes of continuous staying with the three-phase object. But it may be that you have reached the limits of staying that can be developed with the three-phase object, and that a more intricate object is required to trigger more stable, durable staying.

Refining the object of concentration in this way reveals a wider and more subtle range of qualities in the breath, in turn making available to you a wider and more subtle range of qualities of engagement with it. The addition of beginning and end points to the in and out arcs brings delicacy of detail to and a corresponding tenderness of engagement with the object of concentration. Don't worry if your first attempts at this practice seem to upend your efforts thus far. The disruption is superficial. Your underlying practice is not coming undone, you are just changing the terms you are working with, and once that's done, everything will come back together again.

Take up your posture, pick out the three-phase object, and stay with it for a few minutes. It can be helpful to refine the object in steps. First, pick out just five phases, adding only the beginning of the in-breath and the end of the out-breath. Pick up on the first movement of the in-breath, the full duration of the in-breath, the full duration of the out-breath, the last movement of the out-breath, and the felt sense of the breath in the body in whatever interval occurs between the breaths. The first movement of the in-breath has a point at which inhalation begins, a little lift. And the last movement of the out-breath has a point at which exhalation ends, a little stop. Stay with the five phases of the object of concentration for a few minutes, making sure your attention is on the felt sense of each phase and not so much on your naming of them.

Once you are comfortable with this five-phase object, complete the refinement by adding the two middle phases between the in-breath and the out-breath, attending to the last movement of the in-breath, followed by the first movement of the out-breath. The last movement of the in-breath has a point at which inhalation ends, a little stop. And the first movement of the out-breath has a point at which exhalation begins, a little drop. You may experience a slight lull between the two, but they may also pivot about each other so closely that it's more like a transfer of momentum from the end of the in-breath to the beginning of the out-breath, in which they turn about each other arm in arm. You are following the flow of the gestures of the breath, not determining their durations.

The seven phases should be equally distinct in your experience, but they can have very different durations. The end of the out-breath and the beginning of the in-breath are unmistakable and yet seem to have no duration; they're more like punctuation. The interval between the breaths can be variable in duration and mystery. For as long in this interval as there's just the breath in the body, there's just life in its purest distillation, careening along, hands-free. As your practice deepens, that interval will spread out and unfold with greater and greater peace. That interval is the deep well out of which the breath emerges, and into which it vanishes.

Between the end of the in-breath and the beginning of the out-breath, a delicately coupled and airy handoff, with an almost imperceptible moment of ethereal suspension, is revealed, an exquisite brush with the apex of the arc of the breath. The duration of the in-breath and the duration of the out-breath dominate the duration of a single cycle of the breath, complementing each other in a way that can be seen as one thing, its doing and its undoing, stringing together the spectacle of the other five phases.

Like an eddy in a river pool, the in-breath circles upstream and the out-breath circles downstream, the two of them gently orbiting each other as the river flows by.

This variability in the quality and duration of each of the seven phases requires that while you are staying with the object of concentration as a whole, you are also pliantly following it through these phases, with no change in poise. The description of the phases as distinct is intended to un-blur the object of concentration, to make it more crystalline, but the phases are distinct by description only. The pliancy you are developing is the fluid transition from one phase of the breath to the next, circularly, while remaining aware of distinction.

Give yourself as much time as you need for this refined object of concentration to become familiar, for the cadence of the phases to become placid and smooth, for the staying to become relaxed and stately. Refining the object of concentration in this way serves to dispel any complacency that may arise in tandem with your new-found skill at placing and staying. It provides you with a richer context within which the character of concentration may shift. For whatever periods of staying you can maintain, open to the mind's capacity for recognizing the quality of absorption with the object of concentration—a quality that can come both from the object itself and from your deepening involvement with it. Pick up on the felt atmosphere of your concentration for the depth and allure it imparts to your practice.

REFINEMENT CARRIES you into a domain of concentration not commonly experienced outside of practice. It shifts concentration from a relationship you intend with the object of concentration to something akin to mutual entrancement: your mind and the object of concentration jointly constellated, drawn to each other. Your mind knows this relationship already. This is its ecosystem; you just have to open to it and, in doing so, give it the room to flourish.

As a technician, I thought the metrical detail of this practice would finally give me something substantial to work on, but it also happened to inflame the fires of my exactitude. I focused with mordant determination on those specific markers: the first movement, the last movement, and so on. The result was not good. In time, I exchanged pinched striving for an expansive approach by transforming the practice from one of specific detail into one of general detail while retaining meticulousness. I worked with attending to the object of concentration "in that kind of detail." I let go of identifying the phases while maintaining the experience of the intricacy and delicacy of them.

The exchange of specific precision for qualitative precision in this way renders the practice recursively beautiful; when you think you have found all the detail the object of concentration has to offer, look again for the detail within that detail. The closer you look, the more there is to recognize, and the detail may emerge newly minted each time. You also start to get used to your experience being leafed apart into distinctions finer than the granularity of vocabulary, resolved instead into hermetic intimacy.

The experience is not so much one of specific details as one of detailed-ness—detailed-ness in the object of concentration and detailed-ness in the quality of the state of your mind. That object can shift in character and come to entrance. It is not a problem if you find the experience of this practice occasionally delightful. In addition to acting as a lodestone to guide you, the object of concentration turns out to have loft, to have the buoyancy to carry you along on its own.

Return to your posture of stability and alertness, eyes downcast and partially open, spine straight and supple, and attend to your breath, to the felt sense of the breath in the body. Then shift gently to attending to the seven-phase object. As the qualities of this refined object of concentration start to radiate, let the pleasure of them enrich and enliven your practice so that, more and more, all you have to do is feather your canoe back into the stream to carry on. Regard practice as the business of setting up the conditions for the mind to do by itself what it not only knows how to do by itself but wants to do by itself. Practise frequently and for not too long, until some interval of staying with this refined object of concentration is detectable in your direct experience.

Physical pliancy

There is much more to come, but at this point, you may begin to be supported in your practice by the draw of the practice itself. You can be confident that with intent, you have the ability to pick out the object of concentration in the midst of the totality of your experience, and that staying with it is more a question of letting staying happen than striving for it. Added to these natural abilities of your mind, you now have at the centre of your practice an object of concentration of transfixing quality, glittering hand in hand with an opulent quality of concentration. You are reacquainting yourself with the heart of being alive.

Recognizing what your mind is up to as well as the quality of the state it's in is not a conceptual ability. It may initially be experienced as such, since the conceptual mind will leap into action triggered by the recognition of state. But this recognition doesn't start in thought, since thought has abated. This recognition of state is an instance of the mind's awareness of the mind itself, metacognitive awareness, in action. Your practice will reveal this ability to you, since it has been there all along. Just as you recover your physical posture without giving it a thought, there is a plumb line running unerringly through your practice that starts to pull on the practice itself.

This refined object of concentration can provide a further support. Every now and again, breathe with your whole body. Visualize drawing your breath in, clear and bright, from the tips of your fingers and toes, from the entire surface of your skin, from the apex of your skull, towards which your posture is reaching. As you do, let the in-breath reenergize your body and limber up your posture. Then radiate your breath out, soft and warm, from the innermost core of your solar plexus, throughout your flesh and bones. As you do, let the out-breath release tension, unravel knots, and bring ease to your balance. Drop the visualization and return to the object of concentration with your whole body now in thrall, the posture itself inspired.

As your practice unfolds, revisit your posture now and again to develop physical pliancy by comparing your posture to one of the classical ones and making adjustments toward a closer approximation to the ideal. Physical pliancy is a facility that comes naturally to the body. We live and move in our bodies in patterns of habituation, settling into the natural physical strictures of the body, animated by the coursing of emotion. Concentration practice injects a new component into that animation, a component of poise, liveliness, and unfetteredness.

Concentration practice is not some interlude away from life, it's an interlude woven right into life, the life you are living in your body; it will reverberate throughout your body, rewiring how you hold yourself and move; it writes on the body, just as all of experience does, leaving its own original and indelible imprint; it will do this subtly and ambiently in the form of barely noticed shifts and migrations of physique; it may occasionally do this pointedly in the midst of practice on the cushion, in the form of little tremors, jolts, and unravellings. Take careful inventory of your body now and again to keep in touch with how physical pliancy is autonomously reanimating you.

Intensifying

Once you are handy with continuous absorption with the refined object of concentration, staying for several minutes at a time with the felt sense of the breath in the body rendered in delicate detail, allure, and loft, explore the effect on your practice of the level of intensity you are bringing to concentration.[1] What does this mean? If refining is about scrutiny and detail, intensification is about energy. Return to your practice and, with the object of concentration hovering in intricate detail, bring your concentration to bear upon it with laser-like energy: really look at it, intensify on it, on each of its seven phases.

I was taught two exercises for throwing into relief the mind's natural ability to bring energy to bear upon concentration. The first is to hold your arm straight out in front of you, the hand relaxed. Slowly make a fist and clench it for a few seconds, then relax it again. Now do everything you just did exactly as you just did it, but without actually making the fist; leave the hand relaxed. This time, pay attention to the intention, the mental exertion that intends clenching, even as you don't enact it. Notice that you still go through with the clench and release, but they're just the mental trace of the physical action.

The second exercise is to pick out an image across a room and look at it.[2] Now imagine the chosen image is one of those contrived images that transforms into another upon closer inspection. Look at your chosen image like that. Look at it to see whether it isn't actually the image of something else. Pay attention to the mental exertion, the mental leaning-into you muster to bring greater attention and focus to bear upon the observed image, to look for more than you are already seeing.

Once you have played with these exercises enough to familiarize yourself with what it feels like to intensify your concentration, return to your practice as usual and bring to bear the tools you already have—placing and staying, and refining—until you can manage several minutes at a time with an intricate sense of the breath in the body. Let the object of concentration do some of the work for you by drawing you in, entrancing you a little.

Then intensify your concentration on the object as though you were pressing in close to it and lighting it up with the beam of your attention. Use the slightest onset of distraction, the first impulse to diverge, to trigger intensification. Experiment with gently applying this energy, first lightly and then with increasing swiftness and intensity. Keep your metacognitive awareness in place just enough to pre-empt distraction at the very moment it stirs, and to notice the changes in your experience of both the object of concentration and the whole context of your practice. Post your metacognitive awareness like a sentinel, remote but watchful. Spy on yourself. Intensify as much as you can on the object of concentration, really "burn with intensity."[3]

These first practices with intensifying are just experiments with the facility to acquire some skill with it and become familiar with its dynamic range. Keep these exercises brief. There is no general use for a great deal of intensity. What you are after is the skill of calibrating it to arrive at just the right balance. Intensifying is always balanced with its opposite, easing up. You are developing pliancy in the application of the two and a sense for the delicate needle of your internal concentration meter, which will stabilize at just the right degree of intensity.

. . .

While intensifying can seem effortful, consider another description of this practice, which is to "get close to" the object of concentration.[4] For this approach, I'll introduce an example of bringing imagination to bear, to animate and inspire the practice.

The image I use for getting close to the object of concentration is one of standing on the open deck of a sailing ship in full sunshine, sails cracking in the wind, ropes taut and humming, the clamour of voices flying in all directions, the crew bustling with activity, the scene one of excitement, noise, and commotion. Then I imagine descending to the deck below, and the next, and the next, leaving the mayhem above me behind, my footsteps on the ladder steadily becoming the only sound as those on the open deck recede into the distance. The solid wooden beams and the darkness within the hull replace the high-strung masts and spars in the broad daylight on the open deck, the world shrinking into this closed, warm, dark space. As I descend, the silence, the stillness, and the solitude increase, and the presence of the imperturbable keel lying full in the depths becomes palpable. Finally, when I have fully descended and am right up against the keel, everything above is mere spindrift, and below, its thrum in my bones, is the one great timber under way.

Create your own imagery for this deepening, focusing, narrowing process of intensification (or use mine, if you like), and return to your practice as usual. Bring the full power of your imagination, as sensual and emotional as you care to make it, to carry you as close to the object of concentration as you can get. Then drop whatever visualization you have come up with and stay easily with concentration just as it has become.

Eventing

One of the consequences of intensifying in this way is to burn off some of what you take the breath to be. You peel back the named appearance of the breath to get at the occurrence of the events from which the named appearance is derived. Refinement and intensification have brought you up against the unelaborated "fleeting movements of the mind" from which appearance comes forth, also known as "mind-moments."[5] This noun carries with it both the implication of a thing and the implication of a duration, and I got all involved looking for both.

To free myself from the rigours of searching, I exchanged the noun "mind-moments" for the verbal "eventing" to describe a quality of an object of concentration that has been traced right back to the moment in which its occurrence arises.

Return to your practice and become so closely absorbed in the object of concentration that you find yourself engaged with the actual occurrence of the breath, the event of the breath, the eventing of the breath. This eventing of the breath is a more self-sustaining object of concentration than the seven-phase object. It is still the physical sensation of the breath in the body, still a kinaesthetic sense, but intimate enough that it is experienced as much as an event as a sensation. When eventing shows up in your practice, ease up on the intensity just enough for the concentration to begin to flow by itself.

Finding this flow is the true purpose of intensification and easing up. From now on, see the eventing of the breath in the body as a continuous flow, a hovering beacon of pure occurrence. Watch it occur here and now, this, without a past and without a future.

As so often in this practice, this shift to a continuous flow of occurrence is a subtle but distinctive one, a shift in the quality of your experience. It's not something you make happen. Rather, by pliantly balancing intensifying and easing up, you set up the conditions for this flow to show up in your own direct experience as a result of practice. This flow will be the object of concentration from here on. For you to make shifts in practice like this, and recognize them for what they are, an experienced and capable teacher is invaluable.

This pliancy with the energy of concentration is more delicate than other forms of pliancy. To get an even flow, you will be varying intensity through a narrow range. Pliancy with intensity enables a general facility with energy regulation, but while the other pliancies you have been developing will come pretty much to self-regulate, energy regulation, like vigilance, must be a continuously active component of practice. Vigilance is the broad, global component, energy regulation the detailed, specific one.

To set a sailboat on a course, the sailor must, in every moment, combine a global task with a specific one. The sailor must be broadly attentive to every trace of the wind as betrayed by the telltale, the chop, and the flickering shadows on the water, the scudding clouds, the whispering of the air on the sailor's skin and in the sailor's hair, and the momentum playing out through the boat. Simultaneously, the sailor must delicately and specifically regulate both the tiller and the sheets so that in the midst of the dipping and dodging of the wind, the sailor tunes the rudder and the sails just so, not only to stay on course but to do so without a whiff of luff. This same interplay of vigilance and energy regulation will come eventually to reside in the very bones of you, the voyaging practitioner, to maintain your momentum and your bearings, and to keep you unerringly on course.

. . .

THE IMAGES of the keel and, earlier in this chapter, the plumb line evoke the sense of an inherent balance point already beckoning—you just have to home in on it. Once you have some experience with carefully piloting your practice into this natural flow, you will have found your way into the deeper channel of your being. Not only can you then bring this flow readily to your concentration practice; you also can easily turn to it off the cushion, and there it will be, without a lot of fuss and bother.

Every now and again in your daily life, whether in times of composure or times of upset, home in on the sense of an abiding, imperturbable current lying in the depths, the deeper channel. Watch how everything else can be left to skitter about on the surface like leaves in the wind.

Dullness and excitement

The easing of the named appearance of the breath can have a moderating effect on the impact of appearances in general, and you may find your practice taking place in a more amorphous mental environment. The structuring that distraction was providing, unwelcome as it was, did have an orienting effect on where you thought you were and what you thought you were doing. When this effect slackens, experience continues to flow by as you sit, but it does so more amiably.

There's the opportunity now for real endurance in your practice. Endurance comes less as a result of stamina from your side than as a result of integration from the mind's side. As the fidgety limbs of the senses flail themselves out, the mind gathers and turns effortlessly around its own centre of gravity.

But there's also the opportunity for a couple of opposing influences to creep in and impair the quality of your practice. These are the complementary pair *dullness* and *excitement*, both of them impairments to clarity.[6] If intensity influences the depth of concentration, dullness and excitement influence its scope, its clarity. Dullness is a blurring of clarity; excitement is a scattering of it.[7]

Another definition of these is that dullness is withdrawal of the mind inside, experienced physically as drowsiness, and excitement is the scattering of the mind outside, experienced physically as agitation.[8] Perhaps an analogy would be helpful.

Consider following a dew-laden trail through the woods at night with a flashlight that has a loose connection, so the light sometimes dims, sometimes brightens.[9] As you walk along, you keep the beam of light focused on the trail. You are not distracted, nor are you inattentive; you are alert to what the beam of light is illuminating. But when the light dims, things get a little mellow. It's kind of pleasant, and you do not lose your way, but now you are missing the detail in what has fallen into shadow. On the other hand, when the light brightens, things get a little dazzling. The light creates flare on shiny objects on the trail. It's kind of pretty in a twinkly way, but now you are missing the detail in what has been washed out by the glare. When the light is just right, all the detail in the trail is equally clear.

In concentration practice, when the balance of energy is just right, you are neither lulled nor excited by the experience of the object of concentration. Simple clarity prevails, and the flow of concentration is like water coursing smoothly within its channel. With dullness, the water becomes clouded; with excitement, it starts to bubble.

Only as a result of the development of your practice can you become aware of these two flaws. They are otherwise pretty much the steady state of ordinary mind, one of the many ways we have of avoiding direct engagement with mind. Recognizing dullness and excitement, and adjusting for them to restore clarity, require you first to spot these effects to which you are otherwise fully accustomed. You need a refined experience of the object of concentration to throw these flaws into relief, and in correcting for them, you are working with the mind with a delicacy and at a level of detail you have, in all likelihood, never experienced before. You should be proud of the sophistication of your problems at this point.

FAULTS in both vigilance and metacognitive awareness can also cause dullness and excitement. In the case of vigilance, if your attentiveness to the object of concentration slackens, distractions you might otherwise shed start to jostle vaguely on the periphery, drawing away energy and creating dullness, but oh so comfortably. On the other hand, if your attentiveness to the object of concentration becomes strained, your practice will become precarious, and there'll be jitteriness in maintaining it.

In the case of metacognitive awareness, if your attentiveness to the state of your mind becomes diluted, your practice may meander, drifting from its natural trajectory, comfortable but useless. And if your attentiveness to the state of your mind becomes anxious, you can become so closely involved with that state that you distort it in the process, creating vaguely hallucinatory side effects that have nothing to do with anything.

Tuning these two, vigilance and metacognitive awareness, to keep the flow of concentration clear and light is the simplest way of preventing the onset of either dullness or excitement. Detailed and subtle discussions of strategies such as these can be found in the traditional literature, so rather than expanding upon them here, I offer another analogy.

The flashlight analogy is a visual one, and there will be lots of visual imagery to come, but it suffers from tempting the practitioner into looking for actual visual experiences of what are meant only as metaphors. A more internal parallel to the experience of dullness and excitement can be drawn from the experience of reading.

Imagine you find yourself a few pages along in a book you've been reading with moderate interest, but you're not quite sure how you got to the page before you. You realize the words were sort of reading themselves to you as you took a back seat. You were still progressing through the book, you weren't distracted, and you weren't thinking of something else. It's just that you became only mistily engaged with the text, leaving the content on the page. This kind of blurring of the reading experience results from dullness.

Now imagine you are reading a mystery and have reached the point where "who done it" is about to be revealed. You are fully engaged with reading, but you have become so taken up with the story that you are reading past the words. Any craft or subtlety in them is lost on you; your engagement is scattered. This kind of disarray of the reading experience is the result of excitement.

It takes quite a bit of skill to detect and recover from the influence of these two faults. If your practice has evolved to the point where you might be susceptible to them, an experienced teacher will be in the best position to identify them for you. The good news is that once they have been pointed out, you can learn to deploy the mind's own capacity for recognizing faults within staying, to detect when your concentration, while continuous, has become too slack or too taut, and adjust for these.

UNLIKE THE SKILLS you've been learning, faults such as these are not susceptible to explicit practice. You have to rely on them showing up in the natural course of your practice, and they will do so with variety in character and degree, depending on the practitioner. Both dullness and excitement tend to impair their own detection, and sometimes you only discover them when someone with experience recognizes them in your description of your practice. On your own, you are more likely just to get used to them, and then you'll really be stuck.

The traditional literature on the nine-stages pedagogy is rich on the topic of these faults in concentration practice—there's an elephant, a monkey, and a rabbit involved—and the commentaries illuminate different characteristics and different levels of these two classic faults, with much to say about everything in between.[10] You should expect any teacher of concentration practice to be well versed in these flaws and able to help you directly and in detail with developing your skill at detecting them.

The added benefit of learning from an experienced teacher in a group of fellow practitioners is that in the experiences of others, you will hear reports of both faults and their antidotes, which will keep you from having to rediscover them all for yourself. Most important in this context are the subtle versions of dullness and excitement (more about these later), which are even more difficult to detect for yourself than these coarse versions we've been discussing. Hearing them identified, exposed, and rectified in anyone's practice is an indispensable lesson for everyone.

Protect

Once you can bring the object of concentration into a stable flow of momentariness, momentary events eventing, you will have come to an excellent place from which to consolidate everything you have experienced in practice so far. Hereafter, practising gets easier, and imagination will become the principal tool for growth and adventure, but you must deploy this tool with circumspection. The power of imagination is a great asset when applied to self-invocation, and a great hazard when applied to delusion, but I'm not sure I can tell you what the difference is.

You will need to be confident in the basis from which you are practising so that imagination as a tool will cause your practice to flourish without derailing it. And you will need to be discerning so that, amidst all the side effects of practice, you can always pick out recognition in your own direct experience —recognition of details and shifts in the object of concentration, recognition of qualities and states of mind, recognition of faults in clarity.

Before the next shift, give yourself a few weeks of practising a couple of times a day with placing and staying, and with refining and intensifying your concentration on the eventing of the breath in the body. Even as the positive qualities that result from practice—such as stability, flow, and ease—become better established, take the opportunity every now and again to play with the different exercises and techniques. Stay handy with them for those times when you need to deploy pliancy in support of your flourishing practice and to weather the inevitable setbacks.

Consider taking a pause here to work with what you have learned so far, for long enough to consolidate your practice, to establish a daily habit of practice as far as contemporary life will allow, and especially to nurture your motivation for and confidence in what you are doing.

6

RELEASING AND SPACIOUSNESS

Your stuff

Out of necessity, the four practice skills we've covered so far—placing and staying, refining and intensifying—require discipline. They require effort to deploy, and they require you to restrain some of your usual habits of mind: distraction, scattering, obsessing, blanking. I've already described, and I'm sure you've already experienced, the way that practice can aggravate not just those bad habits but the intrusion of all six senses, where your mind, with all its thought, self-talk, and imaginings, is the sixth. As you sit there, engaged in a simple undertaking with modest expectations, you may be met by an invasion of distractions out of all proportion to the unassuming scope of the practice. The senses may seem to be jostling with one another to see which can most effectively disrupt your practice, leaving but frail and fleeting moments of engagement with the object of concentration.

Simple practice will dispel much of this disruption, but you are a red-blooded human being, and some of this disruption is your stuff, your personal psychological menagerie populated by, amongst other things, the tectonic forces of heredity, culture, familial entanglement or want thereof, character, history, metabolism, and the capricious dispensation of a gift for life. As a technician, you may have had your head down, your nose to the grindstone, attempting to practise diligently. It may not even occur to you that part of what you're striving against is your stuff.

The traditions, with all their moral certainty and prescriptive ethics, don't seem to me to have a ready response to our individual dramas, the personal life stories we in the West have worked over so extensively, elevated to the level of mythology, and painted all over the walls. These are fabulous creations, but also entangling ones to the extent that they may include disabling features. These are usually damaging influences chosen from the multiple offerings available by way of self-criticism, self-victimization, perhaps even self-sabotage. Or they could be already-broken aspects of the heart, the body, the mind, or the spirit.

Your own story, while animating you, is bound to have hazards and snares such as these, your stuff. For this, you must take radical responsibility, identify it, own it, and undertake to come to terms with it. Whether and how you do so will depend as much upon your inclination to growth and change as upon whatever human arts for the purpose you are closest to by way of temperament and culture. One thing is certain: the cushion is no place for this kind of introspective process, the blandishments of popular books on contemplative practice notwithstanding.

When your stuff is integrated into your life rather than haunting it—not necessarily repaired or resolved, so much as disarmed through self-knowledge—you will be in a much better position to bring the entirety of your experience to your practice. Your stuff can function as grist for the mill rather than as a wrench in the works. This doesn't mean that you have to suspend your practice while you deal with your stuff—although something of a break might be in order—but it does mean being astute about the expectations you bring to practice in general, and to the following practice skill in particular.

Releasing

The capacity of mind that creates the opportunity to practise the skill of releasing is the mind's natural ability to pick up on distraction at the very moment it arises. Catching distraction early creates an opening for you simply to release that distraction instead of attempting to suppress, resolve, or avoid it. Releasing is a skill distinct from the easing up we were doing with intensification. Easing up is an energy-regulation skill. Releasing is a particular attitude towards the content of experience.

The capacity of the mind to pick up on distraction early in its onset has always been there. You are only now becoming sensitized enough to the content of your experience to detect it. Releasing as a skill is difficult to describe, in part because we are usually not aware of the holding that needs releasing. We regard ourselves as subject to, rather than in any way a participant in, the distraction of distraction. So releasing requires you first to consider that something you're up to with the mind is enabling distraction. Releasing is finding the holding, and then not doing that.

Distraction starts out as reactivity arising in parallel with your concentration practice, and reactivity starts out as a fleeting movement of the mind: a negative movement away from something, a neutral movement of blank indifference, or a positive movement toward something.[1] We are not usually aware of these movements until they have elaborated into thought and emotion, distracting us from concentration. But with refining and intensifying, you have conditioned your mind to expose these movements at their inception.

The elaboration of reactivity into distraction is fueled by your own engagement with that first movement of the mind. If that movement can be detected and your engagement with it pre-empted, distraction will expire before it can impair your concentration. Detection is instinctive, not conceptual. It's why we're in the body.

Just as reactivity develops from this movement into distraction, so too does your engagement evolve from simple noticing to full-blown involvement. You will start by detecting both reactivity and your engagement with it late in the game. You will find yourself in the midst of both. Your first experience of releasing will likely be letting go of an identifiable story, a familiar pattern in the way you respond to a distraction, perhaps some chronic worry or doubt or excitement or confusion or laziness. Once the same pattern has turned up a few times, you can more clearly and effectively direct your releasing of this engagement, and with practice you can do so earlier and earlier in the development of distraction.

RETURN to your practice as usual, and bring to bear the tools you have—placing and staying, refining and intensifying—until you can manage several minutes at a time with the eventing of the breath in the body as a continuous flow of occurrence. To your absorption with this continuous flow, bring the intention to detect the advent of reactivity and the intention to release engagement with it before it evolves into distraction. Intention is an expectation, a resolve in favour of a particular outcome, that creates a receptive potential for that outcome to slot into when it does occur.

At the outset, you'll find yourself catching distraction at some point in its development into thought or emotion, but with practice, you will catch that initial movement of the mind closer and closer to its inception. As soon as you sense either distraction arising or your engagement with it, dis-involve yourself from the distraction, release the engagement from your side, and the distraction will follow in train. You are doing two things here: picking up on how early distraction can be detected, and exposing the extent to which your involvement with it gives it energy and causes it to play out. As both of these factors become clearer in your direct experience, you will be able to bring release closer and closer to the onset of distraction until distraction and release coincide, and distraction spends all its time expiring.

Practise first with superficial distractions such as physical sensations, which are easy to spot, each on its own distinctive channel. The most available and revealing physical distraction is discomfort, such as an itch, an ache, or tingling. Try this exercise first with any mild itching or physical irritation you experience. Withdraw your attention to its disturbance, and release your anxiety about resolving it. Recognize that most distractions of this degree of discomfort will subside simply with time. Give up on them, attend more fully to the object of concentration. Without your investment, they will expire on their own. Be careful initially with aches and tingling, and only work with them once you already have some experience with them coming and, more importantly, going on their own. Simply start to hasten their departure by letting them go.

Then take on not so much thought as thinking. Thoughts are the content; thinking is the activity. When you release thinking, thoughts continue, but you do not become involved with them. Eventually, take on the kaleidoscope of your emotions as they colour your world. See whether you can detect your stuff coursing through them, in their spiralling patterns and swerving energy. Only you will know when to be cautious and when to be bold when taking on your stuff.

. . .

ALL ALONG, I have been emphasizing that the object of concentration is the eventing of the breath in the body. Never drop the body. If you do, you will end up with an interior experience of practice, which will resemble an embodied one but will be bereft of the potential for liberation. In this releasing practice, the most certain way to catch your stuff—especially since it is mostly submerged below the horizon of knowing—is through the unerring, twitching, flickering, resonant filaments of the body. Even if your stuff is on the surface, it's more radical and pre-emptive for you to pick it up where it first arises in the body, since that's where it endures.

From a place of calm staying, carefully scan your body, on the lookout for a sense of constriction or holding, a sense of hiding or numbness, but also for just a distinction, any place in the body that feels different from its surroundings. A difference is the site of potential. The gut, solar plexus, heart, throat, and skull are the usual suspects. When you find such a site, stay with it attentively until you sense the opportunity to release whatever it is that's distinguishing it. This all sounds airy-fairy on the page, I know; there's nothing I can do about that. These instructions will only be recognizable to you once you put them into practice to confirm them for yourself. Eventually, all that will be left of your stuff is you.

At this point in your practice, you are usually encouraged to relax. The problem is that in this context, "relax" does not mean relax. At no point in practice is there a time not to be vigilant, and vigilance requires continuous energy regulation. Since vigilance is only a contingent stance with us in the course of daily life, we regard it as active and effortful. But the stance in concentration practice is a self-sustaining and effortless vigilance, the vigilance that is the natural condition of mind, its way of being when nothing else is disturbing it.

Releasing and Spaciousness

As you are scanning your body, for instance, you are doing so from a poised, composed stance of observation that takes in without getting involved, that registers dispassionately, and then lets you bring release to whatever has been detected. It's vigilance that makes all of detection, dispassion, and release possible. Over time, in the course of practice, vigilance becomes more and more a state of exquisite sensitivity and gentleness. It becomes your resting state and takes the slightest inflection to summon.

THE EXTENT to which you can detect your complicity in the energy and aggravation of distraction is the extent to which you can let it go. What you take to be marauding you will fall away once you release attachment to it. There isn't any distraction to which you can't apply a little letting go. Anything you experience as a shackle can be tumbled free in this manner. The importance of letting go is that it will bring an airiness to your practice, even as you maintain intensity. Airiness dilutes the precariousness of intensifying and makes it easier for you to keep your balance.

This gesture of release is simple, but landing it on the mark is not. Not to over-animate them, but some distractions—particularly pathological ones, and we all have them—may flare up and resist even more intensely at the prospect of being sidelined. It is not inhuman to have an unannounced attachment to the most disruptive forces in ourselves. But it's the really rebellious ones that provide the best opportunity for practice. If you can persist and stay patient with and loyal to yourself and your practice, when these most resistant of disruptions eventually release (as they must and will), the energy they unleash can suddenly convey your practice across stretches you thought lay well ahead; you will find them traversed and left behind in a trice.

The early days of my own practice were characterized by debilitating fits of frustration that arose out of my tendency to "do," which, when inspected closely enough, turns out to be a form of conceit. When I had the opportunity to go on retreat, I'd be strict with myself about making the most of this privileged time for nurturing my practice, intent on not wasting a moment. On one such occasion, the first few days unfolded smoothly and productively, and I was flourishing more happily than I could remember. And then I wasn't. I was experienced enough by then to recognize that I had come to a grinding halt, but not any the wiser about what to do about it.

I'm good at persistence, though, and I'd learnt by then how at least to pretend to be patient, so I was able to stay with the practice rather than stomping off in frustration. I would like to be able to say that I learned to "release the doing," but actually, I simply got so worn down that I couldn't sustain it. I suppose we just let go of our stranglehold on each other. I was forced to resort to the most basic elements of my practice for a modicum of composure. But something about that resignation, the relinquishing of striving, and the giving over of myself to whatever was to unfold, finally freed me from the clench of frustration.

When it did release, the effect was remarkable. I was suddenly sitting with peace, confidence, and above all, light-heartedness. I felt as though I'd been propelled with equivalent energy as far forward as I had felt held back by taut frustration. Farther, in fact. Although the episode had lasted for more than an exhausting day and a half, I seemed to have missed nothing. I was following the instructions not as though I were just learning them, but as though they were second nature. It was a rich enough development for me that I felt almost grateful for the awful struggle that precipitated it.

. . .

Releasing and Spaciousness

YOU ARE NOT FIGURING anything out. You are not making sense of anything that has long bedevilled you. You are simply making a one-sided decision not to hold. Once well developed, this practice of release can be brought to bear on any distraction at any point in its unfolding. It doesn't so much stop distraction as neutralize it, and, with time, it will do so at the first flicker, perhaps even before the distraction has a chance to take on an identity. You will only notice this in hindsight, but there can come a time when you recognize distraction for what it is at the first squiggle and, caught in the act, it releases of its own accord. This transformation of an apparent impediment into an opportunity for recognition and release is famously known as "mistakes arise as wisdom," a description that did not initially strike me as reassuring.[2]

Return to your practice with the eventing of the breath in the body as a continuous flow of occurrence for a few minutes. Take up some incidental distraction that shows up in any one of your senses, something niggling you by way of sight, sound, or sensation. The perverse thing about this practice is that your attempt to be casual about re-engaging a distraction may make it a lot stickier than it was before you made an issue of it. Don't worry. You have some mileage on you now. You can afford the risk of exacerbating distraction a bit in the interest of reaping the even greater assurance that will accrue to your practice once you become familiar with the gesture of release from your side.

With the intention to release it, take up whatever distraction you have selected, take a moment to recognize the extent to which its stickiness is due to you holding on to it, and then let it go from your side. Reclaim the energy taken up by the attention you had invested in it, and replant that energy squarely back in your absorption in a continuous flow of occurrence. The distraction hasn't gone away due to resolution. It has gone away because you let it go. Or rather, it's still there, but the drag of it has been shed. Practise like this until the transition from distraction to releasing is handy for you, and then take on the body scan and, gently, see whether you can handle whatever stuff you find embedded there.

From the beginning, balance doing with allowing. Don't worry about losing anything as a result of this practice. It will all be waiting there for you when you get back. Anxiety, blame, confusion, shame, conceit, obsession, anger, resentment, fear, craving, depression, and the like are deep investments not about to be scoured away by this small gesture of release. This is temporary truce-making, not resolution. You need at least to have taken responsibility for your story to be able to acknowledge the push and pull of it, and to agree to an occasional stand-off with it in order to create a clearing for your practice, and to create the room to breathe, if only for a few minutes at a time. When that story is allowed to encroach once again, you may find that something of this clearing starts to withstand the engulfment.

In time, letting go of everything but the object of concentration will pile energy and depth into your concentration practice, and it will start to hum along on its own. It's called "practice" for a reason: it requires repetition, frustration, dedication, exhaustion, light-heartedness, and a determination to find inspiration every step of the way. The only thing you will consistently be offered is the opportunity to give up.

Your task is to set aside all those things you think you don't have and are striving for, in exchange for everything you are and do now. A certain amount of exhaustion and frustration might even be necessary for you to start learning to balance overdoing with letting go, to start looking to inspiration when every other strategy ends up walling you in.

As you become proficient with releasing, your dependence on whatever alcove of circumstances you have come up with for hosting your practice on the cushion may also ease. You may find that your sitting practice is more adaptable and portable than you thought, and you're quite able to sit in less than perfect conditions. You can take your sitting practice with you when you travel. You can sit when you have ten minutes to wait in the dentist's office, when you take a break on a park bench, or at your desk in class or at work.

Take a moment to let your environment recede and subside. Peek in on it as though you weren't there in person. Find instead your breath in your body, bring your full presence into its presence, and then just ebb and flow on its tide. The pliancy you are developing with releasing is a lot like forgiveness, so it can be difficult to get used to, but it's the perfect practice to take off the cushion. In the course of your daily life, keep an eye out for flares of reactivity, have a look at the dynamic at work there, and see whether there isn't an opportunity to just let something go.

Protect

You may by now be noticing some practical things about your practice. Longer sits, greater ease with the posture, quiet of mind. I don't want to overdetermine your experience by inflaming expectations, but a word about the experience of liberation might be orienting.

If freedom is the goal of practice, liberation, in my experience, is the incremental process of arriving. At the outset, it might show up as unwelcome noticing of your reactivity, a sense that you are not living your life at your will so much as constantly wriggling about in it. This is liberating in the sense that now, at least the trap is in view. As your concentration practice evolves, this experience off the cushion can slowly transform into one of some degree of detachment: your reactivity will still be arising and unfolding, but you will have more of a sense of surfing it than being driven by it.

Well into the practice, liberation can show up as resolution—still the arising of reactivity, but now unfolding without manifesting in conduct, subsiding soundlessly, leaving calm where there might have been entanglement. Liberation also unfolds on the cushion in the form of feeling more at home there: greater ease and depth of absorption, perhaps a certain sweetness that comes from having that kind of time with your mind. Acknowledge and protect these shifts that liberation is leaving in its wake. The more you notice them, the more they will occur, and you will come to see that this process of liberation you are nurturing has a momentum and cadence of its own.

OTHER THAN RECOGNITION in your own direct experience, there are no signposts to the progress of your practice, but I'm going to suggest some metrics anyway, since they can help to structure and support your practice until, in time, it stands and unfolds in its own way. Even though you know metrics are artificial and mean nothing, they can provide a sense of accomplishment at those times when nothing else in the practice seems to be going your way.

Throughout the evolution of your practice, the quality of any particular session is far more important than the duration. As a rough rule of thumb, at the outset, work with an interval of about ten to fifteen minutes, and then take a break. One moment of recognition in such an interval, which is long enough for several thousand such fraction-of-a-second moments, is a far greater development than a mere endurance test of any length, no matter how impressive.

Once you can sit comfortably and productively—or at least without irritation—for ten to fifteen minutes, try adding a second interval after a short break of a few minutes. Once you can sit comfortably and productively for two such intervals separated by a short break, try sitting for two intervals back-to-back, perhaps punctuated by the sound of a bell to reduce the tendency to keep time yourself while you're practising, to free yourself from attending much to time at all. For the purpose of these practices, a total of three intervals in any one sit is probably the upper limit at which they will be productive and comfortable for you.

But I would now like to condemn my own prescription. Metrics of any kind are the tyranny of others. Replace them instead with understanding of your practice, scrutiny of your experience, and confidence in your ability to know your own nature. While this all sounds like an orderly progression, it will be anything but. It can be a messy process on the cushion, and a nagging one off it. Nagging means something has been aroused in you that is determined to be heard.

YOUR MOTIVATION heretofore has been shot through with dedication, eagerness, and no small amount of trust that putting any of this into practice is in the interest of your freedom. When you come to dealing with your stuff and learning to liberate distraction, you are enlarging the scope of your practice to include an unsentimental estimate of your own predicament and a readiness to remain equanimous with it, rather than trying to change it into what it isn't but you think it should be. You are resorting to benevolence.

Your predicament is, fundamentally, your humanity, and with this enlarged attitude of acceptance, it can be seen simply as your path. This enlarged attitude is one of compassion, and it arises naturally as you become less isolated within your own story. To extend it first to your regard for yourself, and eventually throughout your conduct, is to extend your liberation into the world.

Spaciousness

With the practice of spaciousness we come to the last two capacities of mind upon which concentration practice thrives. The first of these is effortlessness, the second, spontaneity. To say that you are capable of effortlessness and spontaneity comes across as oxymoronic if you take "capability" to mean "agency." If, instead, you take it to mean "potential," this better captures the idea that these two capacities of mind will emerge of their own accord, as a result of you getting out of their way. The easiest way to enable these two capacities of mind is to shift your perspective from the felt sense of the eventing of the breath in the body to the felt sense of the eventing of the breath in the body *from the perspective of your awareness*. What does this mean?

Return to your practice as usual, giving yourself over to the eventing of the breath in the body as a continuous flow of occurrence. Now, carefully but steadily increase the height, the expanse of your view, simultaneously expanding the scope of releasing so that you are taking in not just what the thinking mind is up to, but the full spectrum of your experience; not just what the thinking mind is up to, but the full context of being; none of it developing into distraction. Take in everything all at once as mere phenomena, releasing it all at once as mere phenomena, without budging from your place of poise and absorption with the object of concentration.

In my own practice, I imagine standing once again on the chaotic, cacophonous open deck of a ship under full sail. I start climbing the ratlines in the windward shrouds, gently canted in toward the mast so that I lie closer and closer to it as I ascend, the masthead light my sole focus and intent. With height, the rigging becomes stark and taut, and the sounds of life on the deck soften, dilute, mix together, and evaporate upwards and outwards. The sky overhead curves down, globe-like, to the horizon at the same time as everything below flattens out into a one-dimensional disc, most of it ocean pooled under the sky. The flashing sun sparkles off the water, glitters in the air, and causes everything in my field of vision to twinkle into kaleidoscopic fragments, tumbling away from representation. The whole business becomes more particulate the higher I climb, while my mind remains intent on the light at the apex. Once at the summit, the vast totality of the view is balanced by its total airiness. Everything is there, and there is nothing to it.

Create your own imagery for this expanding, diffusing, lightening process of spaciousness (or use mine, if you like), and return to your practice as usual. Bring the full power of your imagination, as sensual and emotional as you care to make it, to plant your view brilliantly on the beacon of the object of concentration as you simultaneously let the space above and below flood out limitlessly, like a river released into the ocean. Drop the visualization and stay with concentration just as it has become.

Maintain an even level of energy in concentration throughout the cycle of the breath, even as, between the breaths, you unfold totally for an instant to the now dilute and multifarious spaciousness. Take in everything else, everything the thinking mind is up to in the background, the neutral hum of everything the mind can apprehend. Do this without for an instant losing any stability or absorption with the object of concentration.

I'll refer to this panorama with its diluted sense of subjectivity as "your awareness," as a way of naming the experience of everything the mind is up to, independently of what you are up to with the mind.

Perspectives

At this point in your practice, you need to grasp something essential about practice that will spare you much grief over striving and attainment. With spaciousness, you are practising the first of a beautiful sequence of shifts of perspective. While I've described this first one as "your awareness," I mean in no way to concretize or objectify a thing called "your awareness." Levels or types or models and the like, of mind or consciousness or insight and the like, are solidifying terms for things that have no solidity whatsoever, and the constituents of which no one can discern.

Every such taxonomy is at best a provisional pedagogical framework, and at worst an impoverishing distortion. Worse yet, they tempt the student to locate practice on some ladder of distinct rungs that ratifies some notion of verifiable progress, a notion that simmers with the endless inflammations of conceit and envy. But we are stuck in language and must use nouns to name these shifts, so I'll be referring to them as ways of looking, as perspectives.[3]

So far, your perspective from within your thinking mind is too narrow to take in what we want to start looking at. The intent of spaciousness practice is to shift your perspective from within your thinking mind to the wider scope in which the mind itself can be experienced as taking place. Hereafter, all of practice unfolds as remarkable shifts of perspective that result from different qualities of awareness emerging in your own direct experience as a consequence of practice. It is the encounter with these qualities that becomes the fuel for practice, the wind in your sails.

Releasing and Spaciousness 89

Free yourself from the rungs of any ladder you are clinging to and scaling. Trust instead in your way of looking, your perspective, to throw the qualities of awareness into relief. Not only is there a marvellous range of qualities, but any one of them can shift in your experience every time you sit, no matter how often or in what manifestation you have encountered it before. Spaciousness, this shift to your awareness, can be differently and delicately shaded each time you practise, and every now and again, it can turn up as a completely new experience. Even after sustained practice, you may find yourself saying, "But I have never been here before!"

Descending to the keel closed down the sounds and sights and sensations of the organized chaos on the open deck of the ship; ascending to the heights, to the singular point of the masthead light from whose beams everything else is precariously dangling, opens everything up. From the keel, everything subsides before it arises. From the masthead light, everything expires as it arises. Climbing to the masthead light opens up the space for all that activity to play itself out in an ongoing flow, to spiral away from itself, to float up into the air and become altogether diaphanous.

You are developing pliancy with shifting the perspective of your practice while simultaneously holding the object of concentration stable, orienting, and exclusive. You expand and shift your awareness; your attention stays put. Every time you sit now, start enclosed with the object of concentration and spread your awareness only as spaciously as continuity with the object of concentration will allow. From this perspective, you will find that the more intent skills of refining and intensifying can be sustained and be more sustaining for longer intervals, and the more diffuse skills of releasing and spaciousness throw the object of concentration into increasingly stark relief.

The centre of your practice is, as ever, your one-pointed absorption with the eventing of the breath in the body. There is no difference in concentration, just a difference in context. At the same time as you maintain the poise of your concentration, you will be taking in the view of everything below and everything beyond, all the way to the encircling horizon, all of it lively but unattended to, selectable but not intrusive, the totality of your experience. This is the view from your awareness, the diffuse, world-making context within which your mind is taking place.

Subtle dullness and excitement

With this shift of perspective, the impairments of dullness and excitement become even more insidious.[4] Two factors contribute to the increased threat of these impairments. The first is the breadth and airiness of the perspective. The second is that now, with your skill at placing and staying, refining and intensifying, and releasing and spaciousness, you will be able to sit for more extended periods of time, extended enough for these influences to seep into your practice undetected, especially as you become complacent.

An experienced teacher should be able to recognize not just the presence of dullness or excitement in your practice, but also the degree. You'll likely be able to report explicitly on the coarse versions of these impairments—blurring or scattering of clarity—even if you don't identify them for what they are. Your report might even be a positive one about something like a dreamy calm or a twinkling giddiness, both overt impairments of clarity.

The subtle versions manifest more as a background sense of atmosphere, so they can be elusive. While you may not be able to report on them explicitly, an experienced teacher will be able to detect their smudging influence from overtones in what you have to say. The additional threat of the subtle ones is that you may have something of an attachment to them, so much so that you discount your teacher's identification of them and turn back to the sirens' call. Work with any instruction you are given in this situation to become familiar with the subtle variability in clarity of your practice, and develop the ability to make these discriminations for yourself.

A further consequence of this shift of perspective is that the language of description starts to falter. It falters not because we are in some mystical domain, but because the perspective encompasses the thinking mind, and language is within the thinking mind. It's the business of the thinking mind to construct reality as you experience it, and it does that with language. That's why language has all those nouns and verbs in it. When language is called into service outside of the thinking mind, it can only resort to poetry.

The consequence of this faltering of language extends to recognition. Recognition as an experience will tend, from now on, to be the more inchoate, more speechless version of recognition I described in the introduction as the "internal blip on the radar screen of the mind," recognition without conception. Be prepared to have perspectives and qualities of awareness described one way by your teacher, another way by a fellow student, and yet another by you. An experienced teacher will be able to recognize in your words correlates to the instructions and descriptions you have been given, and so corroborate your experience—even as you describe it in an idiosyncratic way.

WHEN I WROTE in the introduction about the experience of your mind gesturing to you of its own accord, it is this experience of your awareness I had in mind, an experience of all your senses, including your mind, being pervasive and simultaneous. Not an experience that causes any great reaction, but one that comes up like a breeze; everything goes quiet, and the curtains drift in the sunlight. It doesn't cause any great reaction, since its most compelling feature is its familiarity, perhaps a bit like a memory from the last days of your gestation when you were still an ocean of potential, before discrimination had a chance to carve things up.

The difference between those spontaneous, fleeting moments and the sustained experience of your awareness here in practice is that your absorption with the object of concentration not only creates the spaciousness into which your senses can back off and spread out, it keeps that spaciousness from expiring out from underneath you or leading you astray. From your perspective at the masthead light, glimpse the entire context of your awareness briefly in the interval between breaths while remaining involved with that interval as the object of concentration. This is the practice to which the capacity of effortlessness can be brought to bear, the native ability of your awareness to remain continuous by being utterly expansive.

The traditional instruction to enable effortlessness, to let it supplant every last vestige of effort, is to desist from application.[5] Trust that the mind's natural condition is calm abiding, and let it take place by itself. In the interval combining staying with doing absolutely nothing about anything else, let concentration take place.

Eventually, with practice, as the mind's capacity for spontaneity, the last capacity in our list, is finally free from your interference, calm staying will start to unfold on its own. Everything in your awareness that used to threaten distraction turns out to be the context of the practice itself.

. . .

Releasing and Spaciousness

THE CONCEPTUAL MIND is a fabulous place to spend a life, but for all its free-ranging scope, extravagant creativity, and formative power, it can also be an oppressive place. In concocting experience, the mind is specific and governing, even as it may be regarded as unhinged. Step back from the mind that's doing that, let it do that. This is an imaginative leap at first, one propelled by longing and recollection. Releasing is a gateway to spaciousness. Unstitch, unbundle, release your view from within thinking mind. When you let all that go, what's left? With spaciousness practice, shift instead to that within which the mind itself is shimmering.

Spend some time here, nourishing and establishing your awareness as the new perspective from which you will practise. Consider going back to the beginning of the calm-abiding concentration practices and retracing your steps in placing and staying, refining and intensifying, releasing and spaciousness, but now from the perspective of the open space of your awareness rather than from the narrow scope of your thinking mind. The next and final step in the calm-abiding concentration practices is simplicity itself but depends critically on confident identification and direct experience of your awareness as a perspective, so a review would be worth your while.

7

KNOWINGNESS

There is a final shift to bring to your calm-abiding concentration practice to complete the groundwork for the first of the insight practices. It's vital, though, that you have confidence with and continuity of concentration on the eventing of the breath in the body from the perspective of your awareness as developed at the end of the previous chapter. This final shift to "knowingness," to what's known as the knowing aspect of awareness, while distinctive, is one of some subtlety. It's essential to identify this perspective, since we're going to use it as the foundation from which to set out on the insight practices.

Words

I'm about to make liberal use of some words that evade definition: "self," "mind," and "awareness." Debates over the meaning of these words can lead to endless scholastic dithering, but in this book, I do not mean them in a sophisticated way. This book is not about analyzing concepts, it's about describing practices that will lead you directly to what you need to know, practices that will lead you there without any intervening words. These words work here in the service of the practice of practice, not in the service of a philosophy or psychology or theory of practice. So, for practical purposes, I am going to say what I intend these words to mean without also claiming to define them.

By "self," I intend to mean nothing more than that enclosing sense you have of your being that identifies you and separates you from everyone and everything else. Since reactivity is the aspect of self we are concerned with here, "self" can be read as "the reactive thing." This is the only meaning I intend by the word "self."

By "mind," I intend to mean nothing more than the seat of perception, imagination, memory, emotion, and thought: what I refer to as the "thinking" or "conceptual" mind. This is one of only two meanings I intend by the word "mind"; I expand on the second, looser one below.

By "awareness," thus far in the text, I have intended to mean nothing more than the context in which the thinking mind is taking place, what I refer to as "your awareness," although this meaning is just the beginning of what the word will come to mean for you.

This being a practical book, though, what you need to work with is not self or mind or awareness as I or anyone else intends to mean them. You need to work with self and mind and awareness *as you experience them.*

As certain as we are of our selves and our minds, these nouns are grounded in nothing more than our interior experience of them. In practice, that experience is exactly what you need them to mean. Practice works with your experience of your self, your experience of your mind, and your experience of your awareness, not some concept of them.

Self and mind and awareness are the raw material for practice, so all that matters is that you identify your experience of them for yourself. That experience is what practice transforms, what practice liberates. The result is that the meanings of "self" and "mind" and "awareness" will shift as practice unfolds, and only you will know what they come to mean for you.

Even more provisionally, I'm going to refer to the qualities of awareness that emerge as insight practice unfolds. When I refer to these qualities, I am not saying that's how awareness *is*; I'm referring to ways in which awareness can be *experienced*. Spaciousness practice takes the first small steps in this direction by drawing you into an arm's-length experience of your mind that is perhaps a new experience but will become an increasingly natural one as you practise.

From here on, the goal of practice is to draw out, recognize, clarify, stabilize, and cherish these qualities as your experience of them illuminates the nature of awareness in its inexhaustible variety and display. When I refer to "shifts," I'm referring to transformations of your experience of awareness as these qualities emerge, evolve, and become familiar to you. Through practice, awareness keeps becoming.

Your experience of self and mind will change in quality, will shift, will become less rigid and binding, your relationship to them more elastic. While you may be able to talk sensibly about self and mind, the word "awareness" quickly takes on for the practitioner a meaning that can be found in no dictionary. To avoid being drawn into endless sophistication of the meaning of any of these words, make sure that your experience of them is an embodied experience, grounded in your body, not floating in mid-air in some abstract conceptual realm. Your experience of these words in your body *is* the meaning of these words. Embodied experience is your dictionary.

You will be taught in words, but you will only learn from experience. You will follow an instruction according to the meaning it has for you, and your teacher will ask you about your experience. You will fumble with words, use the ones your teacher used, use ones you've heard others use, cobble together something of your own. And just when you think you're unable to express yourself and are making no sense, your teacher will say, "There. That." And, without thinking, you will know.

Language

While words may be inadequate for describing experience, they are essential for describing practice. To describe calm-abiding concentration and insight practice, we need a language for experience in order to formulate both abstract concepts and practical instructions.

This shift to the knowing aspect of awareness is based upon a characterization of experience derived from the vocabulary you will find in the traditions, but it's possible there are subtleties in the original I have been unable to appreciate. This presentation has only to recommend it that it has served me well so far.

This framework is nothing more than a formalism, a speculative description of a landscape concocted solely to facilitate the navigation of that landscape, without professing in any way to define it. The purpose of the following definitions is to enable practice in your life. In the end, the entire framework —characterization, vocabulary, and definitions—will become more obviously the contrivance it is as recognition dawns and unfolds for you. It's just the scaffolding for exploring a domain that can withstand no linguistic description. So here we go.

. . .

The object of concentration practice is the *experience* of the breath in the body. All of *experience* is taken to be a manifestation of *mind*: experience of the body, the senses, thoughts, and emotions; experience of self, phenomena, and time; experience of space and light.

In turn, mind is taken to be a manifestation of *awareness*; awareness is the context in which mind is taking place, what you've experienced so far as "your awareness." So we have the Russian doll of all of experience—including body, perception, thought, emotion, and the entire phenomenal world—within mind, and mind within awareness.

Experience is said to have two aspects: an *appearance* aspect and a *knowing* aspect.[1] Experience can be said to have an appearance aspect in the sense that there is not nothing in experience, and there is something, something to experience. The appearance aspect comprises the multifarious, unimpedable, luminous display of experience across the senses. The appearance aspect is the content maker.

For appearance to be experienced, there must also be a knowing aspect, something to experience appearance.[2] The knowing aspect comprises the astounding activity of building an entire world and sense of being out of that content. The knowing aspect is the meaning maker.

Since experience is rendered by mind, these two aspects can also be said to be aspects of mind. And since mind takes place within awareness, these two aspects can also be said to be aspects of awareness. While the appearance and knowing aspects of mind together concoct the totality of reality, they are vestiges of the basis from which they arise, the ground of awareness.

Insight does not occur *to* you or *in* thought; it occurs *in* awareness, *outside* of language, since language is rooted in the mind.

In the context of concentration and insight practice, to pick out the appearance aspect—of experience or mind or awareness—is to take what's known elsewhere as the event perspective, the perspective from which you have been practising so far.[3] To pick out the knowing aspect—of experience or mind or awareness—is to take what's known elsewhere as the mind perspective, the perspective to which we are about to shift.[4] The use of the word "mind" here needs some explaining.

I've used the word "mind" so far to mean the thinking mind, your mind. But I've found, in both traditional and contemporary sources relating to practice at this stage, the word "mind" is often used more loosely to mean "awareness": the encompassing, non-conceptual context in which the thinking mind arises. Often enough, it's used specifically to mean the knowing aspect of awareness, and that's the way it's being used in the phrase "mind perspective," the perspective from the knowing aspect of awareness.

One rule of thumb, both here and elsewhere, for determining which meaning of the word "mind" is intended in a given context is that when it's described unfavourably, it usually means our old friend the thinking mind, and when it's described favourably, it usually means awareness, in particular the knowing aspect of awareness. From here on, when I use the word "mind," I mean it in this looser sense of awareness, although I'll still use the word "awareness" interchangeably with it. And when I want to designate the conventional sense of the word "mind," I'll now refer to it explicitly as the conceptual or thinking mind.

Further, since the word "mind" is something of a trigger for me, plunging me into both the allure and the snare of conceptuality, I'm going to abandon the term "mind perspective" in favour of the "knowing aspect" to refer to and more accurately evoke the actual experience of this new perspective.

Shift

Returning to practice, since the object of concentration all along has been the eventing of the breath in the body, we have effectively been practising from the appearance aspect. With intensification, we crept up on shattering the object of concentration into a continuous flow of occurrence from the appearance aspect of conceptual mind. With spaciousness, we demoted the conceptual mind to its circumstances within "your awareness" to shift to the appearance aspect of that awareness. We made this shift so that when we go looking to encounter the knowing aspect of awareness, we won't be misled into identifying it with the thinking mind. We are looking instead for something vast and speechless. How will we make this shift to the knowing aspect of awareness?

TAKE up your practice once again, and bring to bear the tools you have to return to rapt engagement with the eventing of the breath in the body from the spaciousness of the appearance aspect of your awareness. Deploy whatever imagery you have come up with for expanding the context of your practice until the conceptual mind is released into the larger context of your awareness, in there with everything else, keeping to itself. Even as your practice is gravitationally based in the object of concentration, release the experience of all occurrence from being based in the mind. Let the experience of the ocean of all of occurrence spread out limitlessly from the appearance aspect of your awareness.

Then, with the gentlest possible inflection, shift your view of the object of concentration from the eventing of the breath in the body *appearing* in awareness, to the eventing of the breath in the body *known* in awareness. Look at the awareness in which concentration is taking place, the awareness that's doing the concentrating.

Become that awareness. Become the register in which the object of concentration is known to be appearing. The moment-to-moment occurrence of the eventing of the breath in the body—the appearance aspect of awareness—becomes the moment-to-moment knowing awareness of the eventing of the breath in the body, the knowing aspect of awareness. Shift your view to that knowing itself, to knowingness.

Another description of this knowing aspect of awareness and this practice is "awareness of awareness."[5] Ask yourself what it's like to be aware. What is the *experience* of awareness like? Attend to the way in which your awareness itself responds to the pull of that question. Can you sense something brilliant, unwavering, and utterly pervasive coupled with appearance? Can you let all of appearance fuel your sense of the knowing aspect of awareness, your sense of the knowingness with which the whole business is aflame?

The more light-hearted an approach you take to this practice, the more it can weaken your association of the expanse of awareness with the mere expanse of the ocean of appearance, with the mere expanse of the mere universe. Freed from association with something that's not infinite enough, awareness pours away without limit. Appearance becomes mere appearance, you recognize the display, and knowing awareness sprawls voraciously, surging into unboundedness. Even if that's not the outcome for you yet, light-hearted practice is good preparation for the quiet joy that can come from becoming acquainted with this radiant knowing aspect of awareness.

This may be a perplexing account given in words like this, and words are likely to drop you into conceptual mind, so read instructions like this as invocations. Take the echo of them into your practice, and don't try to do too much. Stay closely with the object of concentration; now that it's suspended in the totality of your awareness, unattributed, be prepared for it to reveal its own aspects to you, to reveal the buoyancy in which it is floating. Benevolent attention, intimately held and diffusely expectant, can by itself bring about both manifestation and recognition of the knowing aspect of awareness.

"Buoyancy" is a good word, since the shift from the appearance aspect to the knowing aspect of awareness is a shift into greater ease of concentration, into an effortless flow. It can have a delicate sense of emotional and physical lightness. To further enhance this view, pick up on what has come to be for you the beauty of the object of concentration. All that beauty is coming from the knowing aspect. All you have to do is follow it to its source.

ONCE YOU HAVE a sense of picking up the object of concentration from this knowing aspect, deploy intensification even more carefully than before, both to enhance your identification of the knowing aspect and to get closer still to the object of concentration until it resolves from moment-to-moment occurrence of the eventing of the breath into moment-to-moment knowing awareness of the eventing of the breath. From there, ease up just enough for the object of concentration to come forth in a continuous flow of awareness. The continuous flow of moment-to-moment occurrence from the appearance aspect becomes a continuous flow of moment-to-moment knowing from the knowing aspect, a continuous flow of awareness itself.[6]

One of the impediments to recognizing this shift to the knowing aspect of awareness is that you haven't been expecting such ease. With this shift, there can be an accompanying falling away of any engagement with content, any content, and a parallel upwelling of ease and stability. Part of the sense of expanse of this perspective derives from the way in which unweighting the appearance aspect can dilute the elaboration of content, such that content shows up as simple clarity, the clarity of perception before the thinking mind has had a chance to structure it.

The risk of this dilution of content, on the other hand, is that you may find yourself in something of a blank, dreamy place, somewhere in mid-air. You may drift into a perspective that is *in* your thinking mind rather than *from* the knowing aspect of your awareness. The ever-reliable antidote for this error is to re-ground the object of concentration in the body. Make sure that the object of concentration is, at its core, the knowing awareness of that embodied, kinaesthetic eventing of the breath in the body. Stay with content, even as it does not elaborate, by staying with that most indelible content of all, the body.

When your concentration is rooted in the body instead of in the thinking mind, content will tend to come forth with stark clarity rather than recede into dreaminess. The knowing aspect does not mean that you are absorbed in your thinking mind. It means that you are absorbed with the way in which the eventing of the breath in the body is known in awareness. While this perspective is a more open place, a softer and gentler place than your practice has been heretofore, be sure that the object of concentration itself, even as it shifts to a continuous flow of awareness, is still embodied in the breath in the body. Work a little with this exercise, as delicately and gently as you can, and be careful with whatever experience results.

More than any of the practices described so far, these ones for shifting to the knowing aspect of awareness are, in my experience, dependent upon being heard in the voice of experience. They come to life most fully when both they and you are guided by a skilled and experienced teacher who is aware of the state of your practice, has some insight into your temperament, and can point out to you in your own direct experience your encounter with the knowing aspect. With that kind of instruction, you will gain the confidence to develop the pliancy of alternating back and forth between the appearance aspect and the knowing aspect of awareness, moment to moment, to gain stability with both and to find they are an intuitive and complementary pair.

Besides generating stability, pliancy with shifting between these two perspectives will ease the dominance of the appearance aspect, in which the body is the dominating event. And bundled so tightly with the body as to be indistinguishable from it is your sense of self. The recognition of the knowing aspect of awareness is thus the first step in disarming the dominance of the reactive self.

Protect

The reason for first acquainting yourself, during spaciousness practice, with "your awareness" as the context in which your thinking mind is taking place is precisely to catalyze this recognition of the awareness that's doing the concentration. It's easier to see this knowing aspect of awareness once you can stand back from the thinking mind. From the perspective of your awareness, the shift from looking at the occurrence of the eventing of the breath in the body (the appearance aspect) to looking at the knowing awareness of the eventing of the breath in the body (the knowing aspect) is not such a great leap, but you should notice a distinctive shift in the quality of your practice. With intensification from the knowing aspect, the object of concentration can transform from a continuous flow of occurrence into a continuous flow of awareness that is at once delicately precarious and imperturbably stable, like a gyroscope, never flickering from its induced centre of gravity.

Again, the appearance aspect and the knowing aspect are just perspectives. Identifying them does not imply some division of awareness into constituents, although these two different ways of looking can be experienced differently. In particular, the knowing aspect can have a distinctive fluidity and ease that's essential to transforming your concentration practice into an increasingly effortless one, and extending its range and subtlety.

But as useful as the derivation of these perspectives is, remember that all we are doing is coming up with language we can use to describe practice. Not only are these just perspectives, they can't be said to be independent of each other. We came up with the knowing aspect by reasoning that, for appearance to be experienced, there must also be a knowing aspect, something to experience appearance. That reasoning works both ways: the traditions teach that the knowing aspect cannot stand on its own; there has to be an appearance aspect for the knowing aspect to know—the two co-occur and are inextricable from each other.[7]

There will be much more about all this further along your way, especially once you arrive at what are known as the nature-of-mind practices, which are dismissive of dualities of any description.[8] For now, familiarize yourself with the distinctive qualities of these two aspects, and bring your concentration practice to a place of stability, ease, and clarity.

The knowing aspect of awareness is the register in which all of the insight practices will yield up their recognitions, at the heart of poetic speechlessness.

Calm abiding

The knowing aspect of awareness is not some oceanic concoction of your imagination. It is the expanse you can come to recognize in your direct experience when you settle the full capacity of your attention closely and exclusively on the continuous flow of occurrence co-occurring with the continuous flow of awareness, and then have a look around at the context in which all of experience, in all its aspects, is known to be taking place. Nothing has changed, everything is all still there—what's subsided is your reaction to it. With simple intent, now, every distraction can be freed back into the glittering fabric of awareness.

You have arrived at the state of calm abiding, as it is known, the ultimate goal of concentration practice. You have arrived here not because you have practised being calm or because you have practised abiding. You have arrived here because you have practised recognizing the capacities and qualities of your mind, which is naturally calm and abiding.

Spend some time here with this practice, nourishing and establishing the knowing aspect of awareness as the new perspective from which you will practise. Consider going back to the beginning of the calm-abiding concentration practices once again, and retracing your steps through the practices of placing and staying, refining and intensifying, releasing and spaciousness, with this new object of concentration—a continuous flow of awareness, the eventing of the breath in the body as known from the knowing aspect of awareness. Releasing and spaciousness, in particular, to the extent that they catalyze effortlessness and spontaneity, are a rehearsal for all of the not-doing you will need to bring to the rest of the path.

Once you can practise steadily and with self-determination, there are ahead the nature-of-experience insight practices, which I'll write about in the second part of this book, and, beyond those, the nature-of-mind practices. None of these will be approachable without a grounding in the foundational territory we've covered so far, and they all depend on a sound relationship with a teacher you trust, and who trusts you.

. . .

We have shifted. We used intensification to shift from the felt sense of the breath in the body to the most elemental impulse of the breath, a continuous flow of occurrence. From there, we used spaciousness to stand back far enough to be able to look back upon the appearance of the object of concentration in the context of your awareness.

We then shifted to attending with the same absorption to the knowing awareness of the object of concentration, poised there in awareness. With intensification, we shifted from the knowing awareness of the object of concentration to its most elemental impulse, a continuous flow of awareness.

Along the way, you have used imagination sparingly, as a prop for some of these shifts, to be relinquished once recognition showed up in your direct experience. You are not now standing in some imaginary place. You have just unwound the restrictions on what you are willing and able to recognize. You have taken the most trusted and intimate gestures of your mind and used them to tap here and there on the towering walls of your experience and heard echoes of that tapping in the spaciousness in which those walls were raised.

That encompassing space is there to be plumbed. The echoes of your tapping will continue to return to you and, if you listen closely, captivate you with the news they carry from afar. Above all, you will come to see that they do not come from out of the blue. You will have heard them all along. Only now, with these practices, are you able to recognize them for what they are: the heralds of the heart of awareness.

8
PRACTICE

The goal of concentration practice is to establish a stable, pliable foundation of calm abiding for insight practice. While a teacher can corroborate your experience and direct you onwards, you alone must guide and expand your practice based solely upon your subjective assessment of its quality, and on no other metric.

Let your practice find its own way through the sequence of exercises. Try them in the given order, but don't get stuck on any particular one, due either to ease or to difficulty. Do anything necessary to recreate these calm-abiding concentration practices in an idiom that's meaningful to you. They are coming to a very different world, and they won't survive without you learning to transform and translate them into current form and usage.

Always be alert to reactivity as it arises in the body, since that's where it is rooted and where your attention will be grounded. Practise carefully and with patience, building confidence and pliability as you go. Work with the pliancies described for all of the practices. For extra resilience, work pliantly with what the history of your practice will have revealed to be your habitual distractions. Pick them back up where they have fallen away, let them inflame a bit, and then release them. Release yourself from them, and let the energy this exercise gives off deepen and brighten your practice in a declaration of your liberty.

Be dedicated but not dogmatic. Practise without expectation, and every time you sit, something will give. Some gesture of recognition of the natural stability, expanse, and lucidity of your awareness, however faint, will add to the foundation of the calm abiding you are establishing. In this way, from practice to practice, you will never be the same.

Teachers

Choosing a teacher will take some care on your part. The kind of close instruction that's most helpful at the outset is best found in the context of a direct and personal relationship with a teacher who has the time to attend to each individual student's practice. Since the bulk of practice is your own undertaking, you don't need a great deal of attention from your teacher, but regular periods of engaged, insightful instruction over time would best enable your teacher to become familiar with your practice, and give you the opportunity to become confident in both your and their abilities.

Large traditional organizations can sometimes provide opportunities to receive this kind of guidance from delegated teachers. However, for practical purposes, such organizations typically embed those opportunities in the context of an overall curriculum that may not be well suited to the sceptical, secular practitioner, at least not at the outset. You are more likely to find a good fit for instruction in the calm-abiding concentration practices from independent teachers with more local scope and less programmatic agendas. Look for a teacher both familiar with and experienced in teaching the nine-stages pedagogy. This can be a challenge, since concentration practice is seldom thoroughly taught in the West by either traditional or contemporary teachers. As more students expect to be taught from this time-honoured and detailed curriculum, more teachers will offer it, and fewer of both will rush into insight practice before it can be of benefit.

The traditions have it that instruction be freely given, and students support their teachers to the extent their resources permit. As ideal as this arrangement can be, it can lead to unprofessional confusion over who owes what to whom and for what reason. Unannounced and open-ended obligations create the circumstances for the currying and the dispensing of favour, with the accompanying hazards to relationship. Be prepared to pay your teachers a modest fee for instruction, and be cautious about any other commitment that isn't related to learning what you came to learn.

Retreat

Concentration practice never stops deepening. It always has something more to show you. However deeply and continuously you practise, there will always be some heretofore unencountered or surreptitiously re-emergent thread of entanglement somewhere in the innumerable corners of your awareness to pick out and relax, yielding, as it releases, yet another increment of depth and stability, sometimes even exquisiteness. You can return to the concentration practices over and over again as your practice extends into the insight practices and beyond. As you do, the frontier and foundation of your practice will interact and enhance each other, carrying each other forward hand in hand. The quality of concentration the insight practices yield can be superb when they transform the cacophony of distraction into a source of support.

If you are able, in the midst of working and family life, to make the time and find the space to devote to your practice, you are already doing something heroic, given all the demands upon you and alternatives available to you. Even a modest daily practice can bring a suppleness to your life that derives simply from the awareness you cultivate of the potential for your liberation.

If it is possible also to find the time, the resources, and the opportunity to take yourself off on retreat once or twice a year, to practise for a few days at a time in the company of like-minded practitioners and with the guidance of a teacher, your practice will grow by leaps and bounds. You will come away with a surge of renewed interest in, energy for, and commitment to your practice to see you through to the next opportunity for retreat. Any duration, from a few days to a week, is an invaluable investment in your practice. Whether it's residential or not, rural or urban, is not as important as making that kind of commitment to your practice. Whatever you invest in your practice accrues to the benefit of everyone you encounter everywhere else in your life, whether or not you or they are aware of it.

Off the cushion

The outcome of concentration practice should be a stable, spacious, eased-up dwelling upon the moment-by-moment eventing of the breath in the body from the knowing aspect of awareness. Each person will have residual distractions of varying character and energy. All that need to be undisturbed are your balance and absorption with the object of concentration at the centre of your awareness. The periphery may at times be cacophonous, at times tranquil, but you needn't silence it in order to take up the insight practices. In fact, if things are too quiet, there will be no raw material with which to work. What's important is that you be free from distraction by these distractions, not because you have defeated them, but because you have disengaged yourself from them. That's a description of practice on the cushion, but by this point, you have available to you a natural way of carrying your practice off the cushion.

As you go about your daily life now, start to notice the state of your mind, first in hindsight, but eventually in the midst of experience. Your practice will have sensitized you to how the mind serves as a backdrop against which the content of experience is occurring. Recognition of the background condition of your mind tends to occur spontaneously and negatively as you start to notice, usually after the fact, how scattered or riled or dull you were.

Such negative recognitions can bring you up short. Rather than as occasions for discouragement, take them as occasions for growth, for recognizing that practice has seeped into the circumstances of your life and is starting to alert you to all the unknowing you have been caught up in. Remark the state you recognize your mind to be in without condemning yourself for a lapse in awareness.

Once you have a little experience of the spontaneous occurrence of these recognitions, actively cultivate them when you are in the midst of experience. Simultaneously with how you are, notice how the mind is, without intervention or judgement—just notice. This is practice come to life, taking on a life of its own, your life.

Sometimes, experience can get away from you completely, toy with you as though you have no choice but to be buffeted by it. You fly off into a rage, you slump into melancholy, or you are addled by giddiness. To reclaim a modicum of self-determination and liberty from these forces, there is always available to you the breath in the body to turn to and ground yourself in at a fundamental, physical level.

Let yourself be drawn into and grounded by the deeper channel in which the breath is flowing while experience runs its course. Accept your humanity in both its passionate and its equanimous manifestations.

The mundane quality of these off-the-cushion strategies should not mislead you into regarding them as mere adjuncts to practice. Rather, they are the first steps in living your practice, bringing practice fully to life, fully into your life, and, at some point, leaving the cushion behind.

Meditation

Your multiple passes through the concentration practices—from the appearance aspect, from the perspective of your awareness, and from the knowing aspect—should have nurtured in you by now a durable capacity for concentration from which you can explore the insight practices. The task now is for you and your teacher to decide when your concentration is stable and supple enough for you to undertake and benefit from the insight practices. Prefacing the following with the usual caveats about metrics, it might be a workable rule of thumb to say that if you can set up and maintain uninterrupted and fully engaged calm abiding with the eventing of the breath in the body from the knowing aspect of awareness for five to ten minutes at a time, you are ready to begin the insight practices.

It is possible to take concentration practice to extremes of absorption and endurance, but such feats require you pretty much to absent yourself from life, and they result in what appears to the rest of us to be a self-involved undertaking, even as it is professed to be a self-transcendent one.[1] Reclusion is a compulsion few of us suffer, a privilege few can afford, and a hazard few can survive. In addition to relentless exclusiveness, such feats require relentless effort to sustain;

and without insight, they do not undermine the fundamental snare of your entanglement. An instant of lapsed vigilance and you are right back in the swamp of reactivity.

Not being such an adept myself, I'm sure that's not a fair characterization, but the point is to encourage you to keep your concentration practice in perspective: its purpose is to function as the platform for insight practice, the practice that takes your life as the raw material and works with you where you are, as you are, to liberate you where you are, as you are. At the same time as liberation changes everything, it changes nothing. Everything, including you, will be just as it was, no more easy or difficult, no more happy or unhappy, no more splendid or plain, no more or less heart-breaking. You will simply no longer be so easily entangled in any of it.

There are good reasons for encouraging a start with the insight practices as early as possible. The perspective to which they shift you relieves you of much of the effort you have had to bring to practice so far. It also has a stability and durability of its own to which you can give yourself over. The insight practices have a knock-on effect on the concentration practices, easing, deepening, and enlivening them.

Heretofore, you have been using your metacognitive awareness to assess the quality of your concentration, the state of your mind. With calm-abiding concentration practices, you have been working to establish a serviceable state of composure of the mind that is largely, if not exclusively, undistracted. Once you can establish a stand-off like that, you can look at what the mind is like in general, as opposed to the condition it's in. You can look at the qualities of the mind, not just its state.

The state the mind is in is an aspect of experience. The qualities of the mind are aspects of the mind's own nature, aspects of awareness. Insight practice is the practice of attending to your own direct experience for what it reveals to you about the nature of awareness. You don't thereby end up with a description of awareness so much as a sense of it, of its nature and its dynamics.

From here on, I'm going to use the word "meditation" to refer to this deployment of your awareness as a register in which to recognize the qualities of awareness as they show up in your own direct experience. It does not mean conceptualization of any kind, even though insight meditations will be conceptually instigated so we can talk about them and set up the conditions to practise them.

Compassion

In your practice so far, if you have been lucky, you will have been derailed from your path of progress time and again by the eruption of your own reactivity, your inevitable human predicament of reacting with attraction, aversion, or indifference to the stream of stimuli with which the mind pelts you.[2] These three—attraction, aversion, and indifference—are the "feeling tones" that the traditions maintain precede every reactive moment. They are at the centre of, and something of a fulcrum in, the cycle of "dependent origination" in which, the traditions maintain, we are endlessly entangled.[3] They are the point in that cycle after which it's all downhill.[4]

I hope that you have also had a chance to experience, at least occasionally, the sense of liberation that comes from not always being tethered to your reactivity, occasionally not becoming caught up in it. But to become truly free, you have to go the further step of recognizing how your reactivity plays out in the world you share with others. Until you make this connection, you will merely be fussing over your own personal comfort. Yes, your heart needs to be in your practice, but for your complete liberation, it has to be an unfettered heart, not venturing for you alone.

To make this connection is to let go of living inside the barriers made up of everything you take to be yours. To make this connection is to turn and face the other direction, outward across the web of life, in which all our journeys are intertwined. Liberation is not so much about gaining something as it is about giving everything away.

I CAN OFFER no explanation for how I happened to wander into the ambit of these teachings, let alone what made me think I could come to understand them, but I can tell you what came to be the governing and ever-renewing motivation that has turned practice into a way of life for me.

At the outset, my fascination with the prospect of being able to encounter the nature of my own mind—what it must have been like upon inception—was the engine of my dedication to practice, imbued as it was with poignant longing. This turned out to be not a suspect motivation, just an inadequate one.

The traditions have it that the stream of experience is innocent upon arising in the mind, and it is the instantaneous identifications we make in each moment that create all the trouble.[5] Those identifications are known as grasping: tearing something out of its undifferentiated context in order to relate it—positively, negatively, or neutrally—to ourselves. To be attracted to something, to try to claim it, is grasping. To be repelled by something, to try to avoid it, is grasping. Writing something off as of no interest, being oblivious to it, is grasping. This panic-stricken response to every moment of experience then spreads out from ourselves to reverberate remorselessly throughout the entire web in which we have our being, the web of life.

. . .

I REMEMBER A HAUNTING photograph from the 1994 Rwandan genocide, showing an overloaded dump truck brimming with rubble, receding into a razed landscape in which a bulldozer scrapes at the barren ground and a soldier stands masked against the stench. At first glance, the truck appears to be carrying just a jumble of lumber, straw, and clothing until you recognize in the midst of that jumble the body of a butchered woman draped casually, almost elegantly, from the back of the truck. The grisly mutilation of her face is cast into stark relief by the tenderness of the folds in the shrouds bearing the weight of her corpse, and the strange gracefulness of the one languid arm dangling in resignation from what's left of her.

She has been caught up and destroyed in a cyclone of violence against which neither the victims nor the perpetrators stood a chance. A weather system of hatred laid waste to the victors and the vanquished alike, leaving only bleakness and desolation in its wake. Whichever side she was on, however she got caught up in the violence, she is being thrown away. This utter degradation of life, this utter degradation of humanity, is the inevitable outcome of the poison of grasping that starts with the petty anxiousness of the individual but can escalate seamlessly and rapidly into collective horrors.

When I first saw that photograph, I found it so far beyond comprehension as to have an almost miraculous quality, the miracle of atrocity. But the extent to which it struck me as a miracle was also the extent to which I was unable to accept its reality, the extent to which I too was discarding that woman, consigning her to my oblivion. In the face of this photograph, do I have only the choice of despair or fear or anger or incomprehension?

It seems to me that the least, and possibly the most, I can do is look to my own predicament for the way in which my own lack of awareness results in unmediated grasping—not so much so that I can then become saintly, but rather so that I will at least have a moment to own my reactivity before it spirals away from me. And, just as importantly, so that I can come to recognize that every being is at the mercy of this same reactive predicament, endlessly grasping for comfort, understanding, and fulfilment against the ever-receding prospect of satisfaction.

For me, the scope of practice is now this entire web of reactive beings, all of us flailing and elbowing our own way to our own ends. The motivation for practice is to come to a stance of compassion that lets me open not just to my own predicament, but to the predicament of all beings, victims and perpetrators alike.

When my practice strays or becomes dilute, or when I lose heart or interest or hope, I consider the Rwandan woman in the garbage and all the agents of hatred that put her there, and I practise, instead, out of compassion—compassion for myself and my own trying and failing, compassion for her and her deranged tormenters, compassion for the magnificent and appalling beauty of the human condition.

When I bring that image to mind, whatever impediments I think my practice has become mired in drift away like the dust trail behind that dump truck. The air clears, the heart cracks, and practice turns out to be a way to become a part of the beginning of the end of violence.

PART III

INSIGHT

9

TEXT

[A]ll symbolism in all art and religion is mutually intelligible among all men, and ... there is such a thing as an iconography of the imagination.

— NORTHROP FRYE

Interpretation

In my predicament as a secular sceptic living in the midst of the encroaching shadows of the early twenty-first century, I am indifferent to the elaborately wrought traditional formalisms—unmoved by icons, incantations, ornaments, or rituals. But in my encounter with the calm-abiding concentration practices, I came to understand that these traditions possess remarkable knowledge about the realm of the mind. In undertaking these practices according to the traditional pedagogy, I discovered capacities of my mind that had been operating autonomously in the background, but which I had never bothered explicitly to call into service.

When I did, I found myself able to bring my mind into a state in which it could be experienced as an expansive potential rather than as a riotous cinema. The light itself on the screen itself came to the foreground, while the fiction concocted by the intervening film twinkled formlessly. I found myself in the presence of my mind rather than in thrall to it.

For this experience alone, I am deeply indebted to, and full of respect for, the traditions and their treasury of knowledge and wisdom. I realized that if I was to undertake the insight practices, I would have to find a way into traditional texts that would enable me to learn from them while still respecting my secular stance. I had to develop an ear for what was being said and how it was being said, a task to which the critical traditions of the West are particularly well suited.

We in the West are heirs to assaults on idolatry, superstition, and arbitrary hierarchy, accompanied by desperate human carnage. At stake at the centre of those struggles was the proposition that the sole defence against tyranny lies in the unforgiving but imperative call to self-determination. To blithely slip the traces of this heritage would be to squander the opportunities with which it has endowed us, and to betray those whose lives were lost in the forging of them.

While the West may be regarded by some as disenchanted, it can profess by way of counterbalance a rigorous practice of criticism that supplants the hoary embrace of orthodoxy with the sparkling, if at times disorienting, rejuvenation of interpretation. Criticism and interpretation approach a text with the question *How can this be read?* rather than the question *What does this mean?*

Reading is an interaction between reader and text, and for all the apparent transmission from the text, there's a way in which meaning originates with the reader. Reading can be seen as revealing to you what you are bringing to the text but haven't articulated. In this way, reading begins with attribution, and self-determination begins with the word. Reading is the resurgence of meaning; literalism is the oppressive perpetuation of a particular one.

As a reader, don't obey anything. Texts that endure do so precisely because they are multivalent; they can continually be read anew. The world becomes a continuously transforming place when everything written is understood to be in the shape-shifting, regenerative realm of literature. Even—perhaps especially—allegedly revealed texts can become newly vital, even startling, in the hands of an astute and thoughtful reader.[1]

For me as a secular sceptic, approaching such texts in this way has made them more involving and revealing than I had thought them to be. It also honours the centuries of human hope and yearning that went into creating them. Understanding a text in one's own context is the only responsible way to read. By adopting such an approach, I managed to catch enough of a glimpse of what the traditions have to offer to convince me it would be foolhardy not to attend to the words of those who have had their ears to the ground of being for a thousand years.

Reading in this way is also excellent preparation for the moment when you recognize in your own direct experience that the miraculousness of the world is that it *is* a metaphor.

As my practice has evolved, I have maintained an open receptivity toward traditional forms, neither dismissing nor adopting them out of hand, but instead setting aside for the moment the most inscrutable of them, looking at the more approachable to see whether I can tell what they might be about, and not being too shy to acknowledge when something outside of my vernacular creeps into some corner of my practice and settles in, smug as a stray cat curled up on a new-found hearth.

Words

I am going to try to describe insight practice as I learned it, without too much profession thrown in. I am not an adherent and I am not a scholar, so I have had to find words for my description that did not unjustifiably appropriate meanings I have yet to realize and beliefs I cannot say I share. In using an alternative vocabulary, I do not mean to diminish or discard traditional usage. Rather, I mean to demonstrate my respect for it by sticking to words drawn from my own experience that led me in the direction pointed to by the traditions.

Further, rather than rejecting traditional teachings, I consider them as carefully and as closely as I can to see whether I can understand how they either enable or are an outcome of practice. In my experience, this approach unleashes the potential of the traditions and makes me fonder of them, as I see their influence upon my practice.

"Emptiness"—and why I will always enclose the word in quotation marks—is going to take a bit of explaining. I am told "emptiness" is a concept so subtle and sophisticated that no words can adequately convey its meaning. It has occasioned the writing of some of the physically largest tomes in the canon, and disagreements about it have resulted in violent and debasing schisms within the traditions themselves. As a practitioner, I wonder at the usefulness of such an ineffable word, especially since it turns out to be the one thing you must not fail to recognize.

For the nature-of-experience insight practices described in the following chapters, the traditional instruction referring to the nature of experience you are to come to recognize is to "see it as empty." I could hear in that instruction no way for me to proceed that wouldn't have been me making something up.

It was a source of immense frustration when, after having persisted with dedication through the concentration practices, I found the gateway to insight practice blocked by something everyone was pleased to tell me was an enigma.

To continue at all, I needed to come up with a formulation of that instruction that got close enough to the original to be applicable to the context of these nature-of-experience insight practices. The phrase I came up with was "see experience as constructed by mind." For me, this phrase gets at the provisional nature of reality that I find characteristic of traditional descriptions of "emptiness." I took this formulation to my teacher, George Protos, for his consideration. He thought for a moment, provided the subtle but important revision "recognize experience as being constructed by mind," and thereby handed me the keys to the rest of my journey through the insight practices.

What that revision emphasizes in terms of practice is that insight does not occur in the field of agency and knowing—as in "see it"—but rather spontaneously in the field of direct experience, as in "recognize it." And what is to be recognized is not so much what experience is *like*—as in "constructed"—as how experience *is*, as in "being constructed," its nature.

Lest you become enchanted with constructedness itself, note that this is a criticism of experience; experience is to be recognized as *merely* being constructed.

This reformulation has never led me astray, and I trust that it will carry me reliably to the moment when "emptiness" will show up from its own side, and I'll be able to use the word without pretence. Until then, "being constructed" and "constructedness" will have to serve.

. . .

THERE'S one other important word, the meaning of which I understand but the use of which I found distorting to what, for me, is the defining motivation for practice. When the motivation for practice is described as bringing an end to "suffering"—or, even more narrowly, "your suffering"—it greys out the more demanding and less comfortable undertaking of coming to terms with your responsibility for your conduct. Suffering is the consequence of conduct that is entangled in reactivity.[2] Practice takes you to where the roots of your conduct arise in reactivity and exposes them to you unflinchingly.

For me, it is this reckoning with reactivity that is the startling proposition at the core of the traditions, the compelling motivation for practice. This reckoning is not a comfortable experience, and if you have some notion of doing away with suffering, you might simultaneously do away with what is your best opportunity for liberation. Since it's this more bracing encounter that I take to be the motivation for practice, you will not find any discussion here of freedom from suffering, or its usual accompaniment, the pursuit of happiness.

Besides, I find that reactivity compellingly accounts for the comprehensive ruin in which we find ourselves here in the early twenty-first century.

My reading of "emptiness" as "constructedness" and "suffering" as "reactivity" are the two most radical lexical shifts I made. I made these shifts to learn from the teachings and to unleash their full potential in my life. The discoveries I've come upon as a result have emboldened me to accept the risk that, according to some, these shifts may be distortions. My intent is not to revise the canon. Rather, I am describing the portals through which I was finally able to appreciate it. I find these readings fully consistent with the teachings I have encountered so far, and I expect that one day, when my practice is ready, they will fall away in favour of their traditional replacements.

Teachers

Traditional texts repeatedly emphasize the central importance of absolute trust in and devotion to your teacher, but in my experience, there's a more fundamental principle essential to the student/teacher relationship.

Your primary commitment must be an unflinching adherence to the authenticity of your own direct experience, and resolute confidence in your ability to find your own way. It will take loyalty to yourself to describe only what you yourself experience directly, and to do so in your own words, even as the beauty of the accounts of others tempts you to echo them. And it will take determination to keep your eye on what will reveal itself to be your path, and to proceed on that path at your own pace, without being enticed into someone else's standard of progress.

Strengths such as these will make you a stalwart and dedicated student and preserve in you respect for every facet of the traditions from which you are able to learn. A confident teacher should appreciate a discerning, self-respecting student, so attend to your side of the bargain. Re-smelt the whole business in the crucible of your own direct experience. Test the contention that it can withstand all this. Let just this be your devotion.

Such an approach does not exclude respecting and honouring teachers. Rather, it is an insistence on being careful about enabling hierarchy, privilege, and power, the dangers of which we know, at great cost, to be clear and present.

. . .

I HAVE BASED the following presentation of the nature-of-experience insight practices upon the first two chapters of Khenpo Tsultrim Gyamtso's marvellous little book, *Progressive Stages of Meditation on Emptiness*.[3] I've chosen it as a good example of how energetic, subtle, and direct traditional teachers can be when they are at their best.

Do not let its brevity mislead you. It takes in centuries of evolution of thought and practice in its scope and transforms what has been a divisive debate into an integrated and compelling path of practice. As your practice develops, and especially as you come to know the traditions, it will provide a deepening and orienting appreciation of them time and again. It may seem a slim volume and straightforward in its language, but I know of experienced practitioners who return to it repeatedly. Further, you can expect any teacher who professes to be teaching insight practice to be able to teach you the concepts and practices it describes.

I RECOMMEND APPROACHING TRADITIONAL SOURCES, both texts and teachers, in a spirit of enlightened inquisitiveness, replacing doubt with the benefit of the doubt so that you can freely and easily shed whatever does not speak to you, but still be open to the wisdom encoded therein. On my own journey, I have yet to encounter anything worth ignoring. And I have encountered both traditional texts and lineage teachers who will acknowledge, after all, that you can make your way based upon a handful of uncomplicated precepts and straightforward practices.

If you haven't yet wandered into the traditional literature, you are in for an adventure. Remember as you read that these are the people who have been discovering and navigating the mind for millennia, who brought you everything I have described so far—a fraction of the treasures they have to offer. They have practised, through trials and tribulations of mythic proportions, to enshrine every ounce of their wisdom in a vessel spacious enough to house all the insights they have won, and robust enough to withstand the endless brutalizations of human history. They continue to guard and cherish this wisdom with unbounded courage and shocking generosity. If, in places, the traditional literature strikes you as baroque and esoteric, set aside your reservations for the moment and keep your ear to the ground, listening for the knowledge there that is meant for you.

10

STAGES

A serious human life ... can hardly begin until we see an element of illusion in what is really there, and something real in fantasies about what might be there instead.

— NORTHROP FRYE

The nature-of-experience insight practices are nothing less than a confrontation with our certainty about the nature of the self, the nature of phenomena, and the nature of time.[1] They contest the nature of reality. The express purpose of these practices is to reveal to us, in direct experience, the garden-variety delusions in which all of our ruinous reactivity is rooted. As those delusions subside, there will emerge in their place a self-standing equanimity from which we can start to live with integrity and confidence. The insight practices will transform the circumstantial liberty of concentration practice into a sustained, ambient liberty that can inform every living and dying moment.

The traditions, with their love of enumeration, have catalogued stages for various phases of practice, and they have introduced variety into these litanies as schools emerged and, inevitably, started bickering over authority. As a result, you have to read carefully to be sure which stage of which phase of practice is being referred to. By way of the nine capacities characteristic of each stage, we've covered the *stages of concentration* in the first part of this book, and now we come to the *stages of the path*, which structure practice, and the *stages of insight meditation* on "emptiness."

Stages of the path

Meditation, which we'll come to, is the third stage in the sequence known as the stages of the path, the first two being learning and reflecting.[2] The learning stage—which includes listening and reading—emphasizes the importance of a conceptual understanding of the propositions at the centre of insight practice. The reflecting stage encourages a further step of contemplation upon these understandings, not so that revelation will result but rather so that your conceptual mind will be primed for resonance when the time comes for insight to dawn of its own accord, to be recognized.

Learning and reflecting act to condition your perspective in anticipation of a particular view unfolding for you. Meditation is the opportunity to adopt a given view and then do nothing while you remain vigilant for the true nature of reality to show up by itself in your direct experience. The descriptions of the stages of learning and reflecting are worth lingering over.

LEARNING REQUIRES LISTENING to or studying traditional teachings. As someone who is at best deeply reticent when it comes to belief, let alone faith and devotion, I was uncomfortable with traditional teaching forms, both textual and ritual. This initial response of mine to these teachings was constrained by a cultural bias against orthodoxy I come by naturally in the contemporary milieu of secular scepticism and self-determination.

This constraint stood between me and the messages traditional teachings carry. It was not until I had in hand, in my own experience, the proof of the efficacy of the calm-abiding concentration practices that I could approach traditional teachings. Even then, I could only find what spoke to me by a process of careful consideration. I had to come up with a way of reading that both corroborated the glimpses of recognition I experienced in concentration practice and revealed the territory ahead to which the teachings on insight point.

More important than consideration, though, is the attitude of listening. I have found that listening *for* rather than listening *against* produces significantly better results. If I listen from where my practice is for whatever it is I need next, that will shape what I hear. This is unframed but still expectant listening. If I am defensively strategizing to argue and contest, I am merely maintaining my self-satisfied convictions and will hear nothing. If, instead, I'm expecting an understanding to come to light, I'll be receptive and at ease, and I'll stand a chance of hearing something I need to hear.

At the same time, I have tried to let my traditional teachers know that what they see as a Western propensity for questioning arises not from a negative stance of disbelief but from a positive commitment to authenticity.

REFLECTING CAN ACCOMPANY the activity of learning, but it can also be extended more generally throughout your life. You may have found that your concentration practice has already made you more aware of the background busyness of just being. Reflecting can carry on in the background in the same way, as subversive ideas about the nature of reality, niggling questions standing open at the periphery of your mind, debating the nature of your reality. What are they doing there? Why do these particular questions stick? Let them irritate, intrigue, even provoke you. Suspend doubt and see what comes of that. Get a feel in your daily life for how these kinds of reflections might impact your experience, in particular your experience of what you take to be your self and what you take to be external phenomena.

The most reliable material for taking on what you take to be your self is your reactivity. For instance, whenever you notice that something is starting to get on your nerves (not disturbing, just bothersome)—piped music in a store, someone's garlic breath on the bus, a pebble inside your shoe—with a moment's attention, pick up on the self that is reacting and see whether you can identify it and find out how it's managing to get upset.

To take on what you take to be phenomena, dart your gaze from one object to another, resting a few seconds on each. Make the exercise quick and light. Can you notice that when you dart to the next object, there's an instant before it's locked into identification? There's a moment as the mind constructs it into the thing it is. You don't need to press your temples or go to a monastery to reflect. Going about your daily life with the reaches of your mind questioning your basic operating assumptions is the stuff of reflecting.

The work at the conceptual level—the stages of learning and reflecting—is not to realize the nature of reality, but rather to realize the contrivance involved in what you take the nature of reality to be. There is a huge body of traditional literature devoted to arguments exposing that contrivance, and parallel investigations from the Western tradition.[3] You can find an excellent and concise introduction to these arguments in the text upon which I am basing this discussion, and it provides enough material for you to make a good start with the insight practices.[4]

Some of these arguments are intelligent and subtle, almost convincing. Others are just thought experiments meant merely to toy with the received order. However they come across, the essential role of these exercises is to rattle your complacency about what you think you know. Their most productive outcome is a shadow of doubt.

What I describe below as the commonplace meditations are examples of these ruminative exercises, so you'll get a taste of them here. Work with them in a playful and creative way. Muse over them idly out there in the course of your daily life, not just in the formal on-the-cushion context. Be sure to explore the wider literature on this topic, both contemporary and traditional, to make sure the disruption of your complacency remains lively.

EVENTUALLY, bring to your meditation the intellectual insights from learning and the resulting conditioned perspective from reflecting, and explore these practices on the cushion, looking for the flashes of recognition they are intended to provoke. Note that knowledge and understanding arising from learning and reflecting are second-class relative to the evidence of your direct experience arising from meditation.

Learning and reflecting are activities of your conceptual mind. They work to prime the mind for the recognition it will experience. That's what you are trying most to bring about through these first two stages of the path: a mind that, when it turns to meditation, is primed to recognize what the instructions are pointing to. Trust the listening ability of your mind to pick out the instructions that will best suit the conditions of your practice, and leave the others for another time.

Stages of meditation

There are three nature-of-experience insight meditation practices not because there are only three insights but because we as human beings structure what-arises-in-awareness into reality in these three fundamental ways. The result is that the original nature of what-arises-in-awareness is leached out of experience and lost to us. Taking reality at face value alienates us from true nature. The insight meditation practices bring that nature home to us.

While this division into the nature of self, the nature of phenomena, and the nature of time might appear intuitive to us here and now, the history of the emergence of these stages is the history of a comprehensive cross-cultural inquiry into the nature of the ground of being. You are about to retrace, in your own experience, the time-worn path of centuries of sustained practice and scholarship, of struggle and devotion, that left in its wake orthodoxy and schism, reactionaries and rebels. Underneath this tidy curriculum is the torment and tumult of history. This being a human endeavour, it is tinged with sectarian division and doctrinal carping, but don't let any of that delay you; it's just how we are. The imprint of this drama is reflected today in the vivid and diverse display of the ancient living traditions themselves. You owe everything you are receiving to the lives of everyone who has ever practised before you. Taking up these practices implicates you in this timeless endeavour and indebts you to it.

AT THE END of the calm-abiding concentration practices, you were encouraged to develop a contemplative perspective I referred to as "your awareness." I'll repeat the admonition I made then: your awareness is merely a perspective—one of some spaciousness—from which to regard the simultaneous entirety of what the mind is up to.

The indispensable context for these practices is a serviceable mind.⁵ Such a mind is not just one in which thought has abated, calm is present, and stability has arisen. It is, most importantly, one in which the perspective is the spacious context of your entire awareness, the context in which all of perception is taking place, all thought, emotion, and sensation. This less rigidified perspective is essential to the workings of these practices. It is the context in which the thinking mind, the emotions, and all of the senses are available to contribute raw material to the practices.

For most of us, the sense of one's own awareness is more atmospheric than specific, intuited rather than known, only occasionally glimpsed out of the corner of the eye and then lost again. Awareness sometimes shows up at moments of heightened perception when you encounter some thing or some experience so unfamiliar that your senses sort of dissolve together into a single radar, pooling their information, all of them scanning widely and without focus until something familiar resolves.

The insight practices work directly with your experience of awareness. They expand this experience to reveal qualities of awareness that are obscured by the delusion of the reality of reality. These experiential practices will reveal first a nonsubjective quality, then a nondual quality, and then an atemporal quality in your experience of awareness. The outcome of the insight meditations will be the resolution of awareness into its natural state, radically liberated from the sense of your awareness you began with.

The insights these practices yield up occur not in conceptual mind but from awareness. Awareness is not a thing, it's a particular perspective on experience. Make it serve your purposes, but be prepared for practices beyond these in which awareness and everything it becomes for you will itself become the dissoluble object of meditation.⁶

. . .

What I intend to provide is a reader's guide to the three nature-of-experience insight meditation practices, to assist you in finding your way to and through the traditional sources, both teachers and texts. For each practice, we'll consider a progressive sequence of three meditations, beginning with a commonplace one, followed by a couple of increasingly nonconceptual ones.

I am not speaking from realization. I am speaking as a student who has been taught, who is still learning, and who has an understanding to share. What I provide is just the lie of the land, and I encourage you to make your own way with the engarlanded traditions to pick out the extraordinary narrative these sources have to tell in their own incomparable literature.[7]

11

INSIGHT

> [T]he only thing that words can do with any real precision or accuracy is hang together. Accuracy of description in language is not possible beyond a certain point: the most faithfully descriptive account of anything will always turn away from what it describes into its own self-contained grammatical fictions of subject and predicate and object.
>
> — NORTHROP FRYE

With concentration practice you have been developing metacognitive awareness, the ability to recognize the state of your mind, not just its contents. Based on that recognition, you have been developing skills in conditioning the state of your mind into one of tranquillity and stability—calm, abiding concentration. Recognition, to this point, while acting more and more autonomously in the background, has still had a fundamentally cognitive character and has led to cognitive shifts that manifest as skill with concentration practice.

Insight, on the other hand, is recognition with no cognitive component in either its dynamics or its outcome.

You can have no agency with it. It shows up by itself, by way of intimation. To the extent that you have already noticed anything about the quality of your mind, you have already had a taste of insight. Insight is not the recognition of anything in particular so much as the recognition of the *nature* of something, of the nature of awareness, in this case.

Insight arises as recognition, as an identification *with* rather than an identification *of*. It does not occur in the conceptual mind, where it could be mistaken or forgotten. Rather, it's a resolution of awareness out of the mistaken view we have of it, into its natural state. Such shifts may occur comprehensively or incrementally, but even the slightest shift is complete, irreversible, and liberating.

Insight occurs, and thereafter it is integrated into the nature of experience. It is there. It is with. As wisdom. Liberation is a fire lit from such sparks. Concentration practice is liberating to the extent that you become unmired from your reactivity. I choose the phrase "unmired from your reactivity" carefully. Concentration practice does not eliminate your reactivity. It may moderate how your reactivity plays out, but mostly it enables you to be with your reactivity, to host your reactivity rather than be subject to it. Insight practice, on the other hand, goes straight to the root of reactivity and disarms it. Insight practice is liberating to the extent that awareness becomes unmired from delusion, the source of all that reactivity.

The illusion of the reality of reality is the root cause of reactivity, the root cause of grasping. That illusion arises as a result of our alienation from the nature of awareness; we fail to see the constructedness of everything awareness is up to. Insight resolves awareness out of this mistaken view we have of it into its natural state, and in doing so, eliminates the conditions for reactivity to arise in the first place. The traditions have it that all that energy manifesting as your reactivity will still come forth, but it will do so equanimously, without the distortions of attraction, aversion, or indifference. The insight practices will shift the emphasis of your practice from the concentration skills you have been developing to this more general capacity for insight, which, like the capacities of mind with which you have now become familiar, is natural to you, just waiting to unfold and free you.

The insight practices are presented and unfold in a sequence that reflects both the practitioner's own experience and the long history of the emergence of these practices in the traditions.[1] It is the great treasure and accomplishment of the traditions that they have, over two-and-a-half millennia, discovered and recorded this progress and teachings upon it. It is by the most open-handed gesture that they have ended up in your possession. You are receiving something that comes down to you across the centuries and touches upon the very nature of your innermost being, the nature of your mind. Make these teachings prove themselves in your own direct experience, the only place where what they point to can shine forth unimpeded.[2]

With the concentration practices, you were attending to your mind; with the insight practices, you will be attending to your being. Your awareness is the overt fabric of your being. It's what you take to be the evidence that you are. By recognizing the qualities of that fabric, you will eventually come to discern the ground of being from which it is woven.

The further journey to that ground of being is the domain of the nature-of-mind insight practices that follow these nature-of-experience insight practices and lie beyond the scope of this book. To be prepared for those, you first need to get your awareness out from under the thumb of what you take to be reality.

This is going to require a combination of rough-and-tumble conceptual hacking and hewing, along with delicately refined meditative discernment. At the conceptual level, you wrestle, sometimes pointlessly; at the meditative level, you keep patient, detached, abiding watch.

The work at the meditative level is not to achieve a particular state but rather to set up the conditions for the qualities of awareness to show themselves. It's not useful to try to determine states of awareness. Practise, and trust that the qualities of awareness will gradually emerge along the way, like anything else you nurture. Recognition in this context can sometimes be compelling, but more often than not, it is experienced as a distinct but barely perceptible inflection, something glimpsed out of the corner of your eye. You will have to be patient and open at the same time as you are eager and intent. Seize on nothing. Instead, be careful and gentle with your experience.

However brief or extended, disruptive or revealing any insight meditation session is, spend a few moments as you return to your ordinary frame of mind to acknowledge and consolidate your experience so that, beneath your radar, you are adding to your intimate history with awareness. In your journey with these practices, you will be motivated by expectations, and you will be misled by those expectations, but the only way to arrive at an indescribable destination is through a series of misplaced expectations. All you can do is be sure that you are the one managing those expectations for yourself.

Two truths

The central preoccupation of insight practice is with the tension between what the traditions describe as the "two truths": between "relative truth" and "absolute truth," between the way things appear to be and the way things truly are.[3]

Relative reality refers to reality as we experience it. This definition sounds tautological because we regard ourselves as subject to reality. We have posited it outside ourselves. "Posit" puts it mildly. Fully aware that we observe nothing but change, we are dead certain of the nature of reality as incontestable, certain of reality as the original and ultimate fact. We cannot kick out from under ourselves this one last thing we stand on. It is an indisputably concrete abstraction. It is, by definition, that which we don't question.

As deluded as we may be about it, relative reality is not itself an illusion. It is the experiential world we share with one another, albeit each in our own personal rendition. This world is our predicament at the same time as it is our opportunity for liberation. As deluded as we may be about its nature, relative reality has meaning. It says what it means and, most perilously, it means what it says.

The extended and elaborate discussion and re-discussion of relative truth in the traditions incessantly contests the nature of relative reality, not so much to reveal truth as to create doubts, crises, conflicts, and collapse in the purport of reality, out of which liberation can spring. The nature-of-experience insight practices take on three aspects of relative reality: the self as an entity, all phenomena we regard as being "out there," and the deeply ingrained sense of everything occurring within the past/present/future trajectory of time. These practices ask only whether these aspects of relative reality exist *in the way we take them to exist*; that's all. Whether or not relative reality exists absolutely in the way we take it to exist, or in some other way, is both undecidable and unimportant to the undertaking at hand. More on this ontological theme in a later chapter.

Whatever you make of what the traditions profess about the nature of relative reality, the central principle of insight practice is that all of relative reality is an opportunity for liberation.

We are not in search of anything that we aren't already in the midst of. It will turn out that insight practice, especially when you take it off the cushion, thrives on precisely those aspects of experience that were such a challenge to your concentration practice. Insight practice thrives on your predicament. You will know you have really begun to practice when you find you are no longer looking for something else.

The absolute truth, on the other hand, refers to the truth of "emptiness," the truth of the constructedness of everything, the truth that liberates you from your predicament. Unlike relative truth, the absolute truth is not only not a construction of mind; it cannot be grasped by mind, and it cannot be rendered into words. The absolute truth only dawns in insights that progressively resolve awareness into its natural state.

Here is a working proposition about the nature of relative reality with which to proceed with the nature-of-experience insight practices:

> Everything you experience is represented to you by your mind. There is *nothing* in your experience that isn't attributed to that experience by mind.

This is just a proposition, something for you to test against your experience with the insight practices to find the ways in which it succeeds in upholding or fails to corroborate your experience. The intent is not that you should find it true or false, but rather that it should lead you to the right questions.

The intent of the insight practices is to expose the seeming reality of ordinary experience as a seeming reality—the seeming reality of the experience of the self, of phenomena, and of time. In the wake of the insight practices, what once seemed to be the intrinsic reality of seeming reality is revealed in your direct experience to be an adventitious construction of mind. Reality up and down the line can come to be seen as merely an attribute.

You may encounter related formulations such as "everything is empty," "everything is mind," "everything is an illusion," "everything is a dream," but these are not propositions. They are mystical formulations that can result in tremendous mischief when read as written. They can seduce you into regal positions it is tempting to enjoy, and, more dangerously, they can be broadly trivializing, so I recommend working with this more restrained formulation for now.

Note that the proposition I formulated above already has problems: it posits something called "mind," and it posits that mind is separate from what is experienced. It also posits "you," which you may find either inadequate or superfluous, depending on a certain personal level of anxiety. But all it's intended to do just now is provide a fertile platform from which to practise the insight practices. Rest assured that, as it unfolds, insight practice will directly confront the problem of an independent "mind" and an independent "you," but you'll be much less easy to upset by then.

View

Insight practice requires that you bring your perspective, conditioned by learning and reflecting, into the meditation as nothing more elaborate than "a view," "a way of looking"—a mode of insight practice, as Rob Burbea puts it:

> where insight itself is more a *starting point*, a *cause*, more itself the *method*. In this ... mode of insight practice we more deliberately attempt to sustain a "way of looking" at experience—a view of, or relationship with, experience—that is already informed by a certain insight or other.[4]

By adopting a particular view you have cultivated from learning and reflecting, you shift your perspective on reality as though insight into the nature of that reality has already dawned, and then take up the associated meditation. This shift shouldn't take much more of an effort than switching your perspective from a figure to its ground.

ON THE NEXT full moon on a clear evening, find a prospect from which to watch the moon rise. It's best if you are high enough to have an overview of the landscape or cityscape you are in, and an outlook broad enough to take in as close to one hundred and eighty degrees of the eastern horizon as possible. You want to be able almost to sense the curvature from north to south of the horizon before you. Scan that horizon carefully for the first glimpse of the luminous moon peeping into view.

As soon as you spot it, upend your habitual view of the moon rising by adopting the view that it is instead the earth turning into the east that is revealing the moon, standing there motionless in its place in the sky. Take in as much of the curve of the eastern horizon as possible. Feel yourself turning with the earth, riding on the planet as it revolves into the east and drops over the horizon, leaving the moon revealed where it had been hidden behind the turning earth. The effect is most compelling when the horizon and the moon are juxtaposed, the horizon sliding down the moon. As the horizon sinks to reveal the moon, pick up in your body a sense of the colossal globe rolling you eastward into the evening.

You are the one in motion; it is the moon that's standing still. Let it dawn on you that you are both sensing and perceiving the actual, not the apparent, dynamic. You are recognizing in both body and mind the reality of the earth turning, where before, you were taken in by the illusion of the moon rising.

When you no longer need to hold this view, when it's self-evident and self-sustaining, attend to the softness and simplicity of what has happened in your way of knowing. You have just moved heaven and earth, and you did so with your mind. You are recognizing at last the true nature of moonrise as earth-turn, and it has been staring you in the face all along.

Similarly, throughout these insight practices, you will adopt a perspective on reality as if that reality were being constructed in a particular way by mind. You then take up the meditation, setting up the conditions for the corresponding insight to be recognized directly in experience. When insight dawns, the contrivance you began with will give way with a sigh, like a husk falling away in favour of the concealed seed.

ALL THE LEARNING and reflecting are now to be left behind. Take up your meditation firmly enough to be free from distraction, but openly enough to be able to consider how the experience of reality is showing up from the perspective of your awareness. Find an optimal balance of concentration to set up these conditions.[5]

These are called "analytic meditations" and are often cast in terms of an examination, but the verb "consider" better captures the sense of letting things show up as they are, while you do nothing but remain undistracted and vigilant. All of these insight practices are also "affirming negations": something no longer shows up as you have always taken it to be, and, in being recognized for how it truly is, its true nature is affirmed.[6]

While there is nothing overtly conceptual or perceptual about insight, your reaction to it may play out as sensation, spectacle, or emotion. The recognitions insight occasions occur in your being, not in your conceptual mind, so their reverberations tend to manifest in the unmediated channels of the body, the senses, and the heart—but these are ephemeral side effects.

With insight practice even more than with concentration practice, the outcome of recognition is inexpressible. Even so, it may provoke in you, as it has in legions of others, a torrent of words. It turns out that nothing is more written about than that which is beyond words. But as endless and inadequate to the task as all these words are, they serve an essential purpose: to give the thinking mind some accommodating conceptual bearings so that, when this mind intrudes into your practice, as it can't help but do, it may contribute in its own way to recognition, even as it cannot be a party to it.

The meditations

For each of the three nature-of-experience insight practices, I'll describe three meditations of increasing levels of subtlety and detail.

The first will be commonplace conceptual meditations, equally suited to practising on or off the cushion. These are not intended to convince you of anything so much as to call into question the assumptions you are making about the nature of reality. They are intended to create triggers that will alert you to those assumptions at work in your everyday life.

The second will be on-the-cushion meditations—traditionally referred to as "emptiness" meditations—derived from presentations of insight practice in traditional sources.[7] For these, you set up calm, abiding concentration on a continuous flow of experience and then directly examine the nature of experience from the perspective of knowing awareness. The descriptions of these meditations will almost certainly strike you as elusive at this point. While I present them here in an instructive form, these descriptions are meant to be evocative rather than practical. They are poetic invocations of the territory that lies ahead once you can practise calm abiding with confidence and you have found a teacher to take you through the insight practices.

The third will be a further refinement and intensification in which the meditating mind itself is the object of meditation.[8] The shift is to the perspective of the larger context of awareness itself from which to directly examine the mind itself for direct knowledge of the mind itself. Descriptions of these direct-knowledge meditations can provide nothing but an impressionistic imprint; they simply cannot be described on the page, only referred to in the most elliptical way.

The progressive depth of these meditations mirrors the way your practice of insight meditation will evolve from the conceptual to the nonconceptual. You may be able to make a start with the more conceptual practices on your own, but the nonconceptual practices will only unfold fully under the guidance of an experienced teacher. I am describing them here only to give you some sense of their profundity and elusiveness, and to inspire you to go in search of them.

I will also make a shift in the presentation of the practices in this second part of the book. In the first part, I animated the practices a little by describing how to set them up, take them on, and revisit them, and how to work with the corresponding pliancies and capacities of mind. In this second part, the presentation, while still instructive in form, is intended to be just descriptive enough to give you some idea of the variety and depth of the path, and to motivate you to seek out a teacher who can guide you on your way.

Without some experience with practice, it's unlikely the first two meditations will come across as intuitive to most readers, and even with experience, the third, direct-knowledge meditations are almost certain to come across as resolutely remote. When comprehension becomes elusive, let a reliance on inspiration take its place. More words cannot help. Accordingly, as we progress through each of the three practices and each of the three meditations in each practice, the descriptions will become more threadbare, the lie of the land sketchier, and I'll have less and less to say.

Protect

I have already placed some emphasis on reanimating your motivation as a prelude to every sit, and now I want to bookend that practice with some words about the postlude. Insight meditation turns on the elusive experience of recognizing the constructedness of relative reality. Since words are inadequate as a description of this experience, it's even more important now that you close every sit by taking some time to return to your ordinary sense of self in the world, and to watch what it is that slips away as you do.

Use this transition to throw into relief the contrast between your experience of ordinary reality and your growing familiarity with the nature of its underlying fabric. When you wander into shade from sunlight, wisps of the sun's warmth trail you a bit before they fade. Even then, from within the shadows, you know how blue the sky can be. Something of the periphery has shifted. Insight slides the glass blocks of awareness silently past one another in the air in a traceless distillation of clarity. Be still. Attend to and protect subtle gestures of experience such as these. They are the currents and undercurrents of liberation making its way into the ground from which experience arises. The more you notice them, the more they will occur, and you will come to see that

Insight

this process of liberation you are nurturing has a momentum and cadence of its own and is shifting your foundations.

You can further nurture these shifts by taking your insight practice off the cushion: simply adopt and hold the view of relative reality your practice on the cushion has acquainted you with. Anywhere and at any time in your life, relinquish your usual way of being, and let relative reality come forth newly minted. Watch how experience then unfolds for you with openness and freedom. Eventually, these shifts will start to take place spontaneously, and ultimately, all of insight practice will be like this; it will be your constant way of being in the world.

THE OUTCOME of calm-abiding concentration practice should be a stable, self-sustaining, close abiding of your awareness with the object of concentration. The knowing awareness of the eventing of the breath in the body from the knowing aspect of awareness is the trace of the appearance of the eventing of the breath in the body from the appearance aspect of awareness, the continuously dissolving imprint in awareness of a continuously dissolving event in the living, breathing body, over and over again, and yet without repetition.

From now on, to capture the inextricability of these two perspectives, I'll use the phrase "continuous flow of experience" to name the object of concentration. This in no way de-emphasizes its basis in the body, or privileges either the appearance or the knowing aspect of awareness.

The more you train in and enhance concentration practice, the stronger your conviction will be that while it took a lot of effort, care, and attention to get here, it's a natural place—yours to assume, almost familiarly—to take up where you left off so long ago. From here, you can finally make a start.

Compassion

I wrote at the beginning of this chapter that with the resolution through insight of awareness into its natural state, all that energy manifesting as your reactivity will still come forth, but it will do so equanimously, without the distortions of attraction, aversion, or indifference; it will come forth in the form of compassionate conduct. Insight practice is known as the path of wisdom to this resolution.

The traditions have it that this path of wisdom is inextricably intertwined with its own reflection, the path of compassion, in which it is the cultivation of compassion that leads to the resolution of awareness into its natural state.[9] Just as the path of insight is a path of practice, so too is the path of compassion. And in common with insight practice, compassion practice deals with how we are with ourselves and one another in the world. There is a large and diverse treasury of such practices, spanning cultures and idioms and all of human history. The traditional versions tend to be intricate and full of detailed visualizations, and a preponderance of traditional imagery is taken up with elaborate renderings of the personification of compassion. But at the centre of all these practices is just one thing: open acceptance of the human predicament —our own and everyone else's.

A sceptical stance entails, wisely enough, an element of restraint. But restraint can shade into impairment when smugness or anxiety creep in and throw up the shutters of instinctive reaction where instead there could be receptive consideration. The principle of compassion practice is not to mock up some kind of indiscriminate benevolence you'd feel awkward trying to pull off. The principle is to cultivate an enabling emotional inclination of mind, to soften the ground so that compassion might arise on its own.

With calm abiding practice, you have been attempting to release the thinking mind into its context in awareness. In so doing, you have been expanding and deepening the context in which direct experience plays out. You are trying to tune your being so that it will be supple and resonant enough to register every flicker of insight that will play upon it.

Compassion practice takes on the constriction of the heart that results from chronic reactivity. As constriction subsides, the heart too can break open into that same spacious awareness. The heart too is knowing, and its wisdom is the wisdom of compassion. Compassion practice consists primarily of gently tugging on the constraints of your own reactivity and then just releasing them. It's just a turning toward instead of a turning away, so its outcome can be subtle and gentle at the same time as it's unmistakably liberating. It also prepares you to recognize in your own direct experience, when the time comes, that the nature of awareness, as unlikely as it seems just now, is itself compassion.

As my experience with insight practice evolved, I came to understand that only so much liberation would be possible unless, against all my instincts, I relaxed some of my restraint. I came to understand that without compassionate motivation, the outcome of insight practice would only ever be partial. In your own practice, when there does not seem to be much give, be prepared to seek out and give yourself over to compassion practice. Find a form you feel is authentic and compelling for yourself. You can get all liturgical about it if you like. But you can also just get on the bus and look upon every one of your fellow passengers in turn, asking yourself how you would be contending were you in their shoes.

Without compassionate motivation, your practice and your life will be small. For all its apparent gentleness and benevolence, the transformative outcome of compassion practice, by contrast, is fearlessness.

12

SELF

The fact that man produces a concept "I" besides the totality of his mental and emotional experiences or perceptions does not prove that there must be any specific existence behind such a concept. We are succumbing to illusions produced by our self-created language, without reaching a better understanding of anything.

— ALBERT EINSTEIN

Insight into the nature of the self is the primary and pivotal insight practice, the gateway to all of insight practice to follow. It is rooted in radical empiricism and is intended to decisively disarm the central determining construct of being human: the self. And why does insight practice take aim at this simultaneously keenly cherished and anxiety-riven thing? Because all of the ruin we wreak as human beings arises here.

We recount to ourselves the sorry story of human history in terms of particular culprits whom we demonize as the perpetrators of the horrors we inflict upon one another. But the myth of the individual villain is one we construct to protect ourselves from the awful news that the only way to bring about ruin on such a scale is with the witting participation of millions upon millions of complicit human beings. It is the dimming of vision that shrivels the scope of our mutual care and concern, and creates complicity. Unexamined self-entanglement obliterates civil society.

The savaging of our common humanity is insidious and inevitable in the face of fear of the other—the other gender, other race, other creed, other ethnicity—which arises directly from the anxieties of the reactive self. To the extent that the self is preoccupied with identifying threats, selfhood, by its nature, is anxious. In times of peace, we can seem to be innocent enough as a species, but in times of want or danger, in times of strife or passion, we become entrenched in our most furtive selves. The disfiguring plagues of misogyny, racism, sectarianism, and nationalism are rooted in our individual closeted interiors, where the reactive self instinctively amps up the objectification of the other in response to a perceived threat. In no time at all, fear of an anonymous other in a faraway land becomes fear of our neighbour.

Even in times of peace, we still manage to be thoughtless and negligent. All our wanting and wasting, and our ignorance of and indifference to the consequences, threaten the survival of every living thing—all those other others—on this perfect planet we were handed. The "emptiness" of relative reality notwithstanding, that reality is the human predicament. The "emptiness" of relative reality notwithstanding, here we are, fearing, hating, terrorizing, oppressing, and killing each other, despoiling the earth in the process. Our survival instinct threatens to wipe us out.

One of the many challenging propositions of a secular world view is the assumption that there is no ambient benevolence at large in the world in which we need only have a little faith for it to resolve our self-perpetrated catastrophes.

The insight practices, when pared back to their essentials, place the burden of responsibility instead squarely on our own shoulders to become, against all odds, agents of compassion in the sphere of our own conduct.

This is not a be-good, do-good, feel-good strategy for personal reformation. However beneficial the cultivation through compassion practice of benevolent personal qualities, they are still self-mediated and hence still susceptible to the undercurrents of intent. The fundamental dynamic of practice is to transform reactivity rooted in delusion into discernment arising from insight, from wisdom. It is the nature of our predicament that we are fated to choose and to act. The insight practices disarm the distortions with which intent compromises our choices and actions. By revealing the nature of reality, the insight practices clear the ground for compassionate conduct to arise in this world of its own accord. Were you ever to encounter a ground of unalloyed equanimity from which everything arises, how then would you live?

ONCE AGAIN, whereas the calm-abiding concentration practices address regaining freedom for yourself, this first of the nature-of-experience insight practices addresses the more radical notion of gaining freedom from yourself. It's common to find this freedom from yourself described as freedom from suffering, as a source of happiness, ease, and so on—outcomes that can easily become self-interested goals of practice. A more fundamental freedom is freedom from your own reactivity, freedom that disarms the snare without diminishing the perils of living a human life. Such a release is as likely to be disruptive as comforting.

Before I was taught this insight practice, I had misunderstood what the traditions have to say about this self, due to a combination of a poor choice of words in translation—"emptiness," for instance—and, more misleadingly, cavalier interpretations (of which the present text may well be yet another) by contemporary Western commentators who did not hesitate to imprint their own programs on the elusive and susceptible words from the traditions. My first misconception was that insight led to the extinguishing of the self—if not its destruction, at least its dismantling. The second was that insight led to the resolution of the self into happiness. Since neither outcome struck me as particularly likely, I left them there.

By contrast, the formulation I was taught is that this insight practice is intended to reveal the self to us, in direct experience, just as it is—its nature, its constructedness; that's all. Liberation comes from neither the destruction nor the transformation of the self, but from recognizing its constructedness. Insight into the nature of the self creates the opening, at every reactive moment thereafter, to release the reactive entanglement of the self; that's all.

In place of "happiness" or "awakening" or "enlightenment," look only to liberation, the liberation that is the ground that opens up when the self, in any of its myriad aspects, is recognized as being constructed. The only expectation then should be that this self will no longer be the reactive thing it used to be. That's all, but it's everything.

The point of recognizing the constructedness of the self is not to deconstruct the self. It is to liberate ourselves from its reactivity. "Emptiness" of self is not a view with which to relate to other selves or any other aspect of conventional reality. "Emptiness" is a view with which to relate to our experience of self, others, and relative reality. Recognizing the self as being constructed does not relieve us of any responsibility. On the contrary, it leaves us with no excuses. We can no longer slough off our conduct, claiming that's just how we are.

Absolving ourselves from our predicament is the opposite of liberating ourselves. Self-absolution will morph our constructed selves into even more heedless and intractable things, and we will be unreachable in our conceit. Recognizing the constructedness of the self frees us to embrace it, make our peace with it, and tend it closely, since we are the only ones who can moderate the reactivity to which it is so habitually inclined. A serviceable, operational self is essential to an ethical relationship with ourselves, with others, and with the world we share.[1]

Meditation I

To make this nebulous thing we call "self" more susceptible to a thorough investigation, the traditions propose a breakdown of experience into five "aggregates" that can each be subject to conceptual, ruminative, and meditative consideration.[2] When framed in terms of the self, these divisions can be rendered roughly as self-as-body, self-as-emotions, self-as-perceptions, self-as-thoughts, and self-as-consciousness.[3]

This decomposition of the self into aggregates is a pedagogical tool, not a statement of dogma. You may find these divisions unintuitive, or you may find they fail to accommodate some aspect of the self, but you might also find that such protests arise from self-as-anxiety, which covers just about everything else.

We'll consider the first aggregate of self, self-as-body, in this first meditation, and extend the meditation to include emotions, perceptions, and thoughts. We'll leave consideration of the fifth and last aggregate, consciousness, for the discussion of Meditation III.

This first version of the meditation is a classic investigation of relative reality framed as searches within your direct experience for the substantiality and durability of the self; you are looking for an actual entity that is the self. These are all in the form of thought experiments by way of which your reason and your imagination together can tease the self out from the grip of your reactivity so that it can show up in your direct experience as being constructed.

The important outcome is that these exercises should sow the seeds of doubt in your notion of a substantial, durable self. Once such seeds are sown, they can become rooted and nurtured through reflecting—the undirected musing upon ideas that makes up the more general stew of a conscious life—an autonomous process of taking up and setting down the ambient content of your thoughts.

Take this investigation in that spirit. Let it intrigue and provoke. In the stages of learning and reflecting, you are conditioning your perspective to prime the mind for meditation. You are loosening it up to make it more fertile for recognition, less dominating. Once these ideas take hold, you are unlikely to forget to contemplate them, since you are stuck with an unmistakable trigger that instantly brings them to mind: your continuous and habitual reactivity to the flow of your experience. Every flare-up of attraction, aversion, or indifference is an opportunity for you to recognize the insistent self in full flight and consider what its nature might be.

Eventually, you must return to the cushion with your newly conditioned perspective on the self and deploy any one of the investigations into the aggregates-as-self as a meditation. The key insight to arrive at is that the self is unfindable wherever you look. This is insight practice, so you don't search and find that the self is unfindable by conclusion; that's an intellectual exercise. Instead, you search until unfindability occurs in your direct experience, an experience that is as distinct as it is unmistakable. This is not something you do—the investigative meditation, the search, is what you do. Unfindability is something that occurs, that shows up and that you recognize in your direct experience when it does. As Rob Burbea puts it:

> Here we are engaging in a thorough search for the self or for the essence of any thing. Such a search in practice considers and exhausts all the possible places or ways that it might exist, and so reveals that it simply cannot exist in the way that we perceive and feel it to. We see for ourselves and our conviction grows: not only is it unfindable, but it is *impossible* for it to exist with inherent existence as it seems to. In these kinds of practices, the way of looking hunts for, and then exposes the lack of, inherent existence in one or all phenomena. It then works to sustain the view of that lack, that emptiness, as it continues to regard that phenomenon or all phenomena.[4]

Meditate

Return to your practice as usual, easily and stably absorbed with a continuous flow of experience. Expand the spaciousness of your awareness to take in the totality of experience, the neutral hum of everything the mind can apprehend, while remaining imperturbably absorbed with the object of concentration. Now free up just enough of your concentration to allow a background inquisitiveness a little latitude, and begin a fine-toothed search throughout your body for something you recognize as the self. At first, be systematic. Start at the tips of your toes and ascend your body slowly and meticulously, to the dome of your skull, looking, looking, looking for the same thing: the self you take to be yours, to be you.

Your first reaction to this search will probably be conceptual: "Of course my toe is not my self." What you have done, though, is not "looked" but "selected." You've allowed the toe to pop out as distinguished from the totality of experience. Put it back and start over.

The instruction to "look" is much more diffuse than selecting, even as it takes particular focus. It's more like surveying a loose collection of attributes to see whether any of them is a match for that thing you call the self, until nothing survives inspection. It's like the sweep of a radar, flattening and neutralizing the field of inspection so that the squiggles can be seen for what they are, rather than what they claim to be. Take a lighter touch, and look at the experience of the toe at arm's length with everything else. Don't move on until you come up empty, until you not only don't find the self in the toe, you find that it can't be found there. It is unfindable.

Work repeatedly throughout the full extent of the body until you are certain the self cannot be found there, and eventually extend your search to your emotions, perceptions, and thoughts, anatomizing them in whatever way is intuitive for you. Look at all of them in terms of their fundamental constituents, staying with each until the experience of unfindability is assured, over and over again. Examine the identification of the self with all the constituents of body and mind until it is revealed to be just that: an identification, a badge, a mere attribute—unfindable.

Recognize

Since you will be conducting this search again and again, complacency may set in, and your search may become rote and superficial. Should that creep up on you, remember that the indelible symptom of the self is its reactivity manifesting as emotion. Just when you think you have chased the thing into unfindability, check for any telltale reactivity; you can be sure to find the reactive self persisting somewhere. As I wrote earlier, the body is the Geiger counter of reactivity. Get out of your head. Go to your viscera, where the reactive self may still be lingering.

The experience of the unfindability of the self might be subtle, and there may not be a single recognition that alone makes unfindability definitive. The accumulation of many such experiences over time, however, will eventually result in a distinct but subtle emergence of a non-subjective quality in your experience of awareness—an abatement and, finally, a falling away of subjectivity as a way of looking and being. Your experience of awareness resolves out of subjectivity into non-subjectivity.

This resolution of "your awareness" into non-subjective awareness is so pivotal to everything else to follow that I'm going to refer to this experience of awareness from now on as "natural awareness" to encode the reminder that it is no longer "your awareness" we are talking about.[5] The self is no longer the gravitational centre of being. It's just in the mix with everything else, its privilege dismantled. In addition to this non-subjective quality, the remaining two insight practices expand your experience of natural awareness to reveal a quality of nonduality, and then of atemporality.

These meditations on the constructedness of the self are framed as searches for an apparently existent self through all the nooks and crannies of the body and the mind. The point is twofold: to experience the unfindability of the apparently existent self, and to recognize non-subjective natural awareness as a result. There's what's not found, and there's what remains. This is the key: these recognitions arise together. What turns up in this insight meditation is not just a recognition of the constructedness of the self, but also the recognition of the perspective from which this constructedness is evident: non-subjective natural awareness.[6]

INSIGHT into the nature of the self has the potential to expose to us all of our reactivity and present us with the opportunity to free ourselves from it. The traditions have it that the essential dynamic of the self is to react with some flavour of attraction, aversion, or indifference to every experience that impinges upon it.[7] This anxious little engine of incessant subjective evaluation is not just imposing upon us its dreary priorities. It is simultaneously draining the resplendence out of being, leaving us depleted and isolated, fretting over what we have come to regard as ours. This is just what we've done to ourselves. Imagine how our reactivity blights everyone around us, and the world we all share.

If the shift to the knowing aspect of awareness brings ease and welcome relief to practice, this shift to non-subjective awareness can be poignant to the point of heartbreaking. The reactive self is a contortionist that has managed to stuff itself into a tiny straitjacket of experience pilfered out of the boundless, reverberant space of being. It has sequestered itself from an expanse that, as a result of its own anxieties, it fails to recognize. When you relinquish that reactive self, you will be grounded once again in the sea of being from which you have, by nature, never been separate. It is a homecoming, an end to an estrangement you no longer need to cling to. You will wonder at the years you have spent in exile.

Meditation II

The second meditation on the constructedness of the self follows naturally from the spaciousness of the knowing aspect of awareness developed in the final stages of your concentration practice. The insight it yields has been latent in your practice all along. Bringing this insight into view is just a matter of inflection.

Return to your meditation on a continuous flow of experience from the knowing aspect of awareness, using the interval between the breaths to take in the totality of the expanse of your awareness, as before. Let this spaciousness expand as far as it's able, without losing your poised balance on the object of concentration. Take the loftiest outlook you can across that expanse. Visualize backing off to the edge of the galaxy, like a space probe looking back at earth from the remote and empty reaches of space.

Then, from that galactic space, looking back across that vast expanse, see yourself sitting there on the earth, meditating in perfect poise upon a continuous flow of experience in your awareness. Leave yourself seated there. Shed incarnation at the same time as the object of concentration remains embodied. Become space itself. Let this expansiveness persist as the background against which the eventing of the breath in the body is occurring down there. Spot the mortal mind shimmering in absorption, there where you sit on your cushion, tiny on the planet.

When this perspective flickers into the foreground, attend to the embodied mind down there doing the meditation. Hold this view until all of your subjectivity is seen from a great way off, residing in the meditating self, occurring as yourself, being constructed in a non-subjective context. As your experience of your awareness sheds its subjective quality, that sense of existing behind your eyes, of looking out, will resolve into a distinctive, non-subjective experience of awareness as an expansive field rather than as a personal lens.

Now drop the visualization, and stabilize your view from non-subjective natural awareness by repeatedly recognizing your subjective self as an event taking place from the perspective of natural awareness, being constructed by natural awareness. Any precariousness in this experience comes not from any frailty of natural awareness, but rather from your lack of practice with it and from the anxious pull of the reactive self, intent on keeping you from getting away, from becoming free.

As you drop the visualization, pick up on the liberty that wells up when the self is in abeyance. This experience will have a distinctive sense of freedom—perhaps subtle at first, but eventually clear and stable. It will be deeply familiar to you at the same time as you are unaccustomed to it. This sense of liberty can imbue your experience of non-subjective natural awareness with startling ease and beauty. It can bring your body to home in instinctively on a posture of spontaneous poise and calm. You will also recognize this liberty as that which is lost as the self surges back into the foreground.

It should become clear that what you have been regarding so far as "your awareness" is not the same as self-representation. Natural awareness is pervasively aware, even as the self is in abeyance. Become natural awareness without it being a subjective becoming. Relinquish the conviction bundled up in being you, in favour of abiding in natural awareness, until that conviction drops away. Recognize this conviction itself as coming from natural awareness, as just another expression of natural awareness. Recognize that natural awareness can stand on its own. It's always there, even without you attending to it. From natural awareness, relinquish selfing. Recognize that being is not the same as "being me."

Imagine

You were encouraged in the course of your concentration practice occasionally to finesse your struggles and doubts by simply assuming mastery, taking yourself to be an exemplar of perfect calm and poise, and carrying on with your practice from there. This strategy is even more potent in the context of insight practice when you take yourself to be a realized exemplar of wisdom and compassion. To enhance concentration practice, I suggested you evoke some inanimate totem, but for insight practice, imagine yourself as a being who has had long acquaintance with the nature of awareness.

. . .

Long before I came to these practices—indeed, long before I had matured into any kind of self-awareness—I had been taken by the startling beauty and numinous elusiveness of the standing, folded-arm, female figures from the Cycladic Islands of the Aegean, dating from the third millennium BCE. It was not just their striking modernity that baffled me; I had no idea what experience they were meant to express. With their serene, featureless faces, elegantly elongated heads, and tenderly upturned gaze, what could they possibly be looking at? What rapport with the unseen was reflected in their flawless composure? What knowledge had they come upon that so completed their world? How was it that they were at once ancient and eternal and vividly present?

When I came upon the insight practices, it occurred to me that perhaps the rapport these figures embody is precisely that which results from the complete dismantling of constructedness such that the being is seamless with being. Their gaze then becomes one of radiant compassion for those of us who have yet to find our way to this resolution. Whenever I doubt that wisdom is latent in my own being, I assume the composure I sense in these figures, as though they have bequeathed it to me. I take up their poise and their watch, I fold my arms across my chest, and I continue my practice from there.

Rummage around in your experience for someone who stands out for you as palpably imperturbable. These characters can be fictional, imaginary, or real, it doesn't matter much. What counts is that they should seem to you to live from a well of wisdom and compassion. They are the naturally confident, complete, untroubled, and untroubling figures in your life. In coming into your company, they give you back something that was yours upon creation but which you have lost track of along your way. They recall yourself to yourself.

They are a longing fulfilled. In them you find gifts you have known all along, the memory, the experience of which have unaccountably eluded you. How is it that you recognize these gifts? You recognize them because they are of your own nature: confidence, poise, dignity. Beginning here, and as your insight practice evolves, occasionally assume such a privileged stance; become an exemplar of wisdom and compassion, and continue your practice from there.

Protect

This second insight meditation on the nature of the self turns on the imaginative power of the idea of space. It explicitly evokes spaciousness as the frontier of the reach of human imagination, the infinite cosmos, the great beauty of which is that it eludes us. When you drop the visualization of this envisioned perspective, nothing is holding you up other than that which renders both the infinite and the ungraspable.

In the course of your daily life, spaciousness as a cue to this shifted perspective is always at hand. You don't need the circumstances of the cushion to undertake the practice. As frivolous or recreational as it may seem, start taking a moment every now and again during the course of the day to let go of being in the self.

Take up a view distant from where you are, looking back at where you are. Stay with your experience, and then let everything in between fall away, leaving only expansiveness. Relinquish the physical metaphor of "space" for the direct experience of "spaciousness," a quality of natural awareness. Natural awareness is the view from which your experience of infinity is rendered. It is the enclosing context of boundlessness.

. . .

INSIGHT into the constructedness of the self is the pivotal practice for the rest of your way. There's great breadth and variety in approaches to it, and even once you feel assured, it will be worth revisiting again and again. For as long as you practise, the illusion of an independent, apparently existent self—the most distorting illusion of them all—will never rest in its efforts to reclaim its accustomed domination, and it will be endlessly creative in how it attempts to do so. Whenever reactivity is present in life, it's a sign of the resurgence of the self. The enabling condition for practice from now on is to recognize the constructedness of the self, relinquish it swiftly and with skill, and shift to the non-subjective perspective that remains once the self is in abeyance: natural awareness.

It is no longer "you" that is meditating; it is no longer "your mind" that is meditating. The meditation is now *in* natural-awareness-coming-into-its-own. You should be able to feel the difference, the unfetteredness. Take as much time as you need to explore the breadth and variety possible with this practice. Thoroughly root out this illusory self, and become expert at detecting its resurgence.

Eventually, you will find that it's the nature of natural awareness to be poised and imperturbable. Early on, in writing about the development of concentration practice, I described the remarkable experience of not-seeing, of vision taking place even as vision dropped out of your awareness due to your absorption with the object of concentration. The corollary here is that with increasingly complete absorption with the object of concentration from the perspective of natural awareness, the self can come to be not-seen. In releasing and spaciousness practice, especially as the thinking mind is recognized to be the self chattering to itself, knowing can be released from the thinking mind altogether, and the only register of knowing left is natural awareness. The self will be not-seen. The vanishing of subjectivity in this way reveals it only ever to have been a mere construction. Its absence leaves nothing behind but unwavering equanimity.

Return repeatedly to the concentration practices, even as insight develops for you, since those practices can serve indelibly to fortify insight itself. We are not trying to get the self to vanish; it will do that by itself. We are trying to recognize its constructedness as clearly as possible.

You can get excited about insight occurring all of a sudden on the cushion, and when it does, it is often accompanied by compelling emotions and sometimes even a sense of an altered state. Such moments, should they occur, can bring depth and momentum to your practice, but they are not ends in themselves. They arise out of the process of liberation and leave liberation in their wake as they subside. So accept and acknowledge the gift, and let them go. It has also been my experience that insight is mostly gradual, and beautifully so. Pyrotechnics are thrilling, but there's something exquisite about the surreptitious emergence of the dawn.

Whatever degree and kind of recognition you experience in a given sit, take a few minutes to stay with that experience before you rise. Keep your hands off it. Carefully familiarize yourself with where and how you are now. With practice, you will resort to your spacious perspective swiftly, and natural awareness will show up on its own. Thereafter, spend the rest of your time on the cushion "resting" the mind in this perspective.

I've used the word "resting" since that's the word you'll find for this practice instruction in most sources, both contemporary and traditional. However, I have never found "resting" helpful in any practice context. The word dumps me right back into my usual slovenly state of thought, my personal hammock on the porch of life, whiling away the time. I've come to understand that a more accurate phrase is to "let the mind be," which captures the essential point that you continue to maintain your view—with however slight an inflection—but react in no way to the proceedings.[8] It's that lack of reactivity that constitutes the state of rest, even as you remain vigilant. So rather than resting the mind, I hear that instruction as "maintain the view from natural awareness, and let everything unfold in a continuous flow of experience."

Direct knowledge

The remaining two nature-of-experience insight practices reveal further qualities of awareness by undermining your assumptions about the experience of phenomena and of time. But before leaving this first insight practice, it's possible to deepen your experience of the constructedness of the self by adding refinement and intensity to your practice, just as you did with concentration. In the same way that refining and intensifying gave your concentration practice stability and durability, they can likewise enhance your insight practice. You deployed these two strategies when you had a modicum of engagement with the object of concentration. Similarly, once you have regular and sustained experience of non-subjective natural awareness, you will be in a position to bring refinement and intensification to bear, to stabilize the insight even further.

BUT FIRST, it might be a good idea at this point to remind yourself how far afield practice has taken you. Your first step was to extricate yourself from everything your mind was up to, so that you could simply abide calmly with the object of concentration. That took a bit of work. Then, for even more imperturbable staying, you shifted from the appearance aspect of experience in the mind to the larger sense of your awareness as a whole, the context in which concentration was taking place. From there, you picked up on the knowing aspect of awareness to abide with the concentrating mind itself from knowingness itself.

With the surroundings so subdued, the object of concentration, while still the eventing of the breath in the body, became ethereal, rarefied. This knowing aspect became your entrée to the nature-of-experience insight practices.[9] With the first of these, you are unhitching yourself from the domineering perspective of the self so as, in a way, to become natural awareness itself. You are recognizing the constructedness of the self.

Whatever disappointment you may experience upon discovering that nothing about you is immutable should be offset by the beauty of the realization that you are, therefore, invocable.

Once you are familiar with the two remaining nature-of-experience insight practices into the constructedness of phenomena and time, you will be able to abide here effortlessly. As each stitch of all of experience is unpicked again and again, you will have a way of being that has nothing in it but the recognition of constructedness, nothing in it but liberation, even as experience comes forth as it always has. You will have the opportunity at every moment to unfold yourself *with* experience rather than contest yourself *in* experience.

And as accomplished, as wide-ranging, as flexible, subtle, and comprehensive as you become with the recognition of constructedness, just when you think it has run its course, there it will be, another level of gentleness beckoning you, an even more open way to be. When you return, as you must, to your ordinary sense of self, you will begin to experience the expiration of your reactivity even before it has a chance to arise. The leash still jerks, but only catches air. You could not be blamed for living from now on in this way.

Self 175

. . .

BUT THE TRADITIONS PERSIST. Beyond these foundational nature-of-experience insight practices, there are nature-of-mind insight practices and, according to the most ancient and austere of the traditions, yet further practices that refine away every last vestige.[10] All of these are not only well beyond the scope of this book—they are outside my experience. All I can do with the third meditation in each insight practice is recount to you my understanding of what I have read and learned of direct-knowledge insight practices—the precursors to the mind's natural condition of awakened wisdom—if only to give you a sense of what the terrain ahead might look like.[11]

As much as has been written about them, these direct-knowledge insight practices are best learned from an experienced teacher. None of what's written about them can do anything for you other than provide some sense of corroboration after your practice experience has led you to and through this territory. Everything you read about these practices will only ever make sense in hindsight. You can come back to the same few words time and again, and be alternately puzzled, intrigued, or startled, all depending on nothing more than the state of your own practice.

What I'm able to present is, therefore, just a relic of a literature that has long since been unable to say what it means, and yet is specific, detailed, elaborate, and, to the appropriately tempered ear, compelling. I write of these practices only to name the frontier, not in any way to illuminate it.

You will determine for yourself how far along this path you will go before you find yourself living the life you were meant to live. It's possible that the further reaches of this path only unfold for a few: those whose fate it is to become teachers, adepts, lineage holders, human embodiments of the practice.

Whatever your undertaking turns out to be, relinquish any expectation of arrival. Give yourself over to the journey.

Meditation III

While the first four appearance-like aggregates—body, emotions, perceptions, and thoughts—may be characterized as expressions of the appearance aspect of mind, consciousness, the fifth aggregate, may be characterized as an expression of the knowing aspect. This third meditation on the constructedness of the self examines consciousness, in search of an identification with the self that's more subtle than the others, more likely to elude the radar.[12] Consciousness is the fragment of the knowing aspect of awareness that the self has carved out and appropriated to itself.

In the previous nature-of-experience meditation, you were looking at the experience of the self in mind to see whether you could catch mind constructing that experience for you. You did this by trying to identify the self as an entity, a findable thing. When you exhaust the possibility that the self is an entity, you are left with the direct recognition of its being constructed by mind. However, even after all your thorough searching through appearances has determined the self to be unfindable anywhere, there may still be a residual identification of the self with this fragment, the sense of "me" as "my consciousness," the knower.

In this direct-knowledge version of the meditation on the constructedness of self, you refine and intensify the meditation by looking instead at the awareness that is doing the constructing, to see whether you can find the knowing aspect as an entity. You directly examine the knowing aspect of mind itself for knowledge about the mind constructing all of experience. Specifically, in the continuous flow of experience, you first pick up on both the appearance aspect and the knowing

Self 177

aspect of that experience. You then pick out the knowing aspect, as you have practised and become familiar with doing, to see whether you can come to any conclusion about it, whether you can recognize that ongoing sense of knowing itself as having any basis.[13]

The examination takes in any and every aspect of experience as it arises: experience of thoughts, emotions, and perceptions; experience of the body; experience of the mind itself. While the meditation emphasizes the knowing aspect, the appearance aspect is still present as the object against which to detect the knowing aspect.

The engagement with experience is light and peripheral. As experience flows by, be it continuously or in apparently discrete moments, pick up on the mind that knows that experience. Pick up on the registering of experience in mind. Watch as the different sense experiences lose their distinctiveness as you shift to the common knowing of appearance: that which is present with and seems to host appearance.

Where is the mind through which experience is flowing? That sense of continuity is where the sense of self-as-consciousness is arising. Where is the mind that knows this experience? You are examining the knowing aspect of mind, independent of the content of the known experience. Look again to see whether that knowing aspect has any basis in substantiality—in things, in the body—or any basis abstractly—in events, in mind. Examine the mind with mind.[14] Look until the constructedness of the knowing aspect itself is recognized. Natural awareness has the capacity to know without agency.

IT IS SAID that this direct experience of the constructedness of the knowing aspect of mind brings forth the true nature of natural awareness—like space, but with the capacity to know itself.[15] As Daniel P. Brown puts it, the knowing aspect just is:

awareness-itself shines forth of its own accord once obscurations are removed. True knowledge just *is*. It is a property inherent in human existence.[16]

Practise

In summary, throughout all three of the foregoing meditations, the practitioner must test and retest the recognition of the constructedness of the self—and the simultaneous recognition of non-subjective natural awareness—by picking out this most distorting of events, the reactive self, in the flow of experience, and repeatedly searching all of the aggregates until unfindability is the consistent outcome. With each recognition, natural awareness is incrementally stabilized and deepened. Refining the practice in this way is not done to achieve anything. It is not about arriving at natural awareness. Rather, it is about recognizing non-subjective natural awareness as it already is and cultivating the conditions again and again for the recognition of natural awareness to arise unbidden.

For the calm-abiding concentration practices, I went out on a limb and described some of what the experience of liberation might be like. With the same caveats about expectations, I want to extend that description, in the most provisional way, to the insight practices.

With these meditations on the constructedness of the self, there's the opportunity for reactivity itself to show up as being constructed, at arm's length, if you will. Reactivity can be recognized as a symptom of the constructed self, arising from the constructed self, and hence a mere construction. Anger lights up a particularly fierce edition of the self, one deeply invested in the anger itself. If you can recognize the way in which your anger intimately reflects the person you are, then you can see that it's contextual, it's you who's making it up. Without you, your anger has no meaning. It can't get a hold.

A flare of reactivity throws into relief the constructedness both of itself and the self. The two betray each other, resolving into insight.

Further, more so than with the concentration practices, liberation in the insight practices can have a sensual element. The body can come to feel less discontinuous with the world, more integrated with it. When you behold being from natural awareness rather than through the senses, the body is included with all the rest of being rather than separated from it as an observer.

Deepening recognition of the constructedness of the self can result in experience taking on an all-encompassing sense. With recognition of the constructedness of phenomena and time, experience gets even lighter and can take on an all-arising sense. These descriptions may or may not resemble your experience of liberation as you practise, but be alert to and treasure recognition of such liberating shifts in your experience of experience. Don't lay your hands on them. Just be watchful, and they will gently integrate into your being, into how you are.

The insight practice into the nature of the self is the first of the nature-of-experience insight practices because it is the key insight practice. Everything to follow flows from here and is a refinement of the perspective the practice is intended to cultivate: natural awareness. Natural awareness is the catalyst for everything to follow. Everything else is easy. Everything else falls away.

The practice does not destroy anything. It has nothing to say one way or the other about the existence of anything. Its power lies in its ability to change your mind, not so that you think differently—although that will be a natural side effect—but so that your mind itself is changed.

Listen

As I have said, you may be able to make a start with these meditations on your own, but there are good reasons that only hearing them in the voice of an experienced teacher will unleash their full potential.

First, the state of awareness you have been cultivating so assiduously in your concentration practice has a certain liberty from cognitive dominance. Going spacious does not mean going vacant. It means all faculties of mind have a more equal footing than when you are principally thought directed. If you were to be given an explicit meditation to guide yourself, the cognitive activity required would upset this balance. If you were to conduct the investigation yourself, you would already be too busy to hear, and you could get involved in answering, which is useless.

Relieved of that duty by the voice of an experienced teacher, you can just listen to the words of the meditation instructions and let your mind follow them without too much cognitive elaboration. The words can slacken from their given meanings and come forth, lustrous and stirring. You are freer to let your imagination inspire the meditation by trying on the instructions there first so that they can more easily seep into the meditating mind. The investigations these meditations entail ask no questions to which you don't know the answers. They ask questions the answers to which you must experience. The intent of the meditations is to arrive at the direct experience of the "unfindability" of the self, the direct experience of the constructedness of the self.

Further, your cultivated state of awareness has a certain permeability to it, making available to you a register of mind more directly connected to direct recognition. When the meditation is guided in the voice of an experienced teacher, it creates the opportunity for you to hear the voice of experience, and the experience in the voice. I was taught that the mind will jump at the words as though it has been waiting for them. The oral traditions are clearly not oral due to a lack of literacy; the traditional literature is both voluminous and inspiring. That literature makes continual reference to the primacy of the human lineage created by human-to-human transmission, to the primacy of the agency of the spoken word.

For these meditations to be most effective, it's essential that you hear them from a teacher with enough experience to recognize that the quality of your concentration practice is stable enough for you to conduct an investigative meditation of this kind. Such a teacher should be able to guide you through a meditation in which you first establish your meditative equipoise, and then follow the teacher's spoken instructions for searching through every aspect of your own direct experience for a substantial, durable self.

There is no substitute for a guided meditation in the voice of one who knows whereof they speak. Listening to spoken instructions is also excellent preparation for any opportunity you have to encounter a traditional teacher in whom you will hear the sound of this human lineage as it has come down to them across time, and now to you.

Cherish

With this insight into the constructedness of the self, you come to the most significant threshold in your practice. Looking ahead, all the rest of insight practice is catalyzed by taking and holding this perspective of non-subjective natural awareness. Practice can seem to be all diligence at times, a sequence of frontiers that only seem to open into further frontiers. There can occasionally be fatigue and loneliness in this pursuit. So a little cherishing of your practice thus far can serve to embolden the heart to continue the journey.

While the calm-abiding concentration practices may have required sustained effort on your part, when refined, they take the mind to a place that turns the tables on effort, and practice becomes self-sustaining. I suppose there are adepts who come to this stage from the perspective of ordinary self, but in my experience, this kind of poise blossoms most easily and resplendently from non-subjective natural awareness. Over time, your recognition of the self as being constructed becomes more assured as your concentration deepens and broadens on its own. In Rob Burbea's beautiful rendition:

> Eventually we can even come to work with this balance of [concentration] and insight practices in meditation the way a great eagle might ride on warm air currents, skilfully, easefully, and elegantly inclining the direction of its flight as it wills, in subtle and sensitive response to those currents.[17]

Once you have reliable experience of natural awareness, revisit the mind's native inclination to calm abiding by way of placing and staying, refining and intensifying, releasing and spaciousness, imbued with the expanse of natural awareness. When intensifying, descend once again to the keel and settle there, but this time from the point of view of the expanse of the ocean, not the ship. For spaciousness, ascend once again to the masthead light and settle there, but this time from the point of view of the expanse of the sky, not the ship. Practise none of these for long or in a belaboured way, just long enough for you to sense the way they are native impulses of your mind—long enough to come to recognize that you were made for this. Mind inclines toward knowing itself.

Looking back, concentration practice can be lit up all over again, this time from natural awareness, with enough room for everything that used to be a distraction to peter out in the immensity, and with enough momentum for the object of concentration to carry the whole practice by itself from its own side: the natural tendency of natural awareness to stand perfectly still in the light. From this view, re-explore your concentration practice on the eventing of the breath in the body, in the non-subjective context of natural awareness.

On the cushion, with the self in abeyance, concentration can have a stability and a durability otherwise impossible to accomplish. Off the cushion, with the self in abeyance, you can recognize its constructedness when it flares up, and you have the opportunity to take your self lightly, to shrug your self off.

MUCH OF THE FOREGOING—AND indeed much of what the traditions themselves have to say about the self—can come across as an indictment of the self, but your practice will wither in place if that's the conclusion you come to. So, before leaving this chapter, I'd like to bring back into the foreground the ways in which the self, constructed though it may be, is essential to a mature, engaged, evolving, and fruitful practice.

At the outset, I wrote that what's at stake in this endeavour is the freedom to live as who you truly are. At the close of the previous chapter, I wrote that compassion practice takes on the constriction of the heart that results from chronic reactivity, and in this chapter, I've written that the point of recognizing the constructedness of the self is not to deconstruct the self, it is to liberate yourself from that reactivity. I also wrote that recognizing the constructedness of the self frees you to embrace it, make your peace with it, and tend it closely; that a serviceable, operational self is essential to an ethical relationship with yourself, with others, and with the world we share.

So there's a "you" and a "heart" and a "self" here that, once disentangled from reactivity, is at the centre of practice: the self is your human agency after all, and if compassionate conduct is to make its way into this world, it has to do so through us human beings, as ourselves.

While the essential outcome of recognizing the constructedness of the self is to disentangle yourself from the reactivity of that self, I also wrote that that recognition can be accompanied by the beauty of the realization that you are, therefore, invocable. That "you" is the constructed but nonreactive human being you truly are, that can function not just as the vehicle for your liberation but also as the embodiment of compassion. As your liberation deepens and extends throughout your life, the constructed self can gradually resolve into a natural condition of confidence and dignity.

13

PHENOMENA

The world is in some essential sense a construct. Human knowledge is radically interpretive. There are no perspective-independent facts. Every act of perception and cognition is contingent, mediated, situated, contextual, theory-soaked. Human language cannot establish its ground in an independent reality. Meaning is rendered by the mind and cannot be assumed to inhere in the object, in the world beyond the mind, for that world can never be contacted without having already been saturated by the mind's own nature. That world cannot even be justifiably postulated. Radical uncertainty prevails, for in the end what one knows and experiences is to an indeterminate extent a projection.

— RICHARD TARNAS

Ignorance of our true nature, manifesting as reactivity, is not just a snare in which we are caught; it diminishes us by obscuring our full potential. It wrecks what we're up to and keeps us from becoming everything we could be. The instinctive discrimination of "self" from "other" as a fundamental way of being is a species of panic that only elaborates, intensifies, and becomes increasingly anxious moment to moment. It requires that we simultaneously reify the self and objectify the other, and a tremendous amount of energy is dedicated to the project. Reification and objectification are locked in a fraught embrace; no liberation is possible until they both fall away.

You can work at loosening their grip through any one of the heartfelt compassion meditations you will find in all manner of humane traditions. A mature practice is one that expands to look directly at the reactive self and its enmities and actively undermine them. But the cultivation of compassion is the preparation for a more profound outcome. The traditions have it that the recognition of one's true nature carries with it the recognition that everything arises in original equanimity. It all starts out as unalloyed expression, unconstructed, everything all at once, undifferentiated. You don't have to do anything except get out of the way, and it's by way of insight that you dismantle your constructed barriers.

For me, this is the ultimate motivation for compassion practice. You cultivate compassion in your own conduct to foster the conditions in which spontaneous compassion can arise of its own accord, manifesting as conduct consonantly integrated with the conditions of your life. As contested as the reality of the world will be in this chapter, what remains unchanged is that this is a world we all share; it is our predicament. And, as I was taught, in this world, conduct is everything.

Meditation I

For insight practice, I described an optimal level of concentration at which examination and analysis still operate.[1] In the context of constructedness-of-self, the latitude allowed in concentration needed to be just enough for the ordinary sense of self to be taken up and regarded at arm's length.[2]

In constructedness-of-phenomena practice, you extend that latitude right out to encompass all of phenomena as presented to you by sense perception constructed by mind.[3] This is extremely loose perception, barely an appreciation of sense, bereft of elaboration. Your basis is still the imperturbable object of concentration: some incarnation of the eventing of the breath in the body, anything from physical inspiration to mere "moment-iness."

Whatever form the object of concentration takes, it's the unwavering support upon which this meditation unfolds. You are in a stable place to do this, given your confidence in and pliancy with concentration, combined with recognition of the constructedness of the self. If "self" is clearly a construct, who is there to become distracted? Distraction turns out to be one more faulty engagement with an expression of natural awareness. Once the constructedness of the self is recognized, its privilege is dismantled, leaving everything else in experience on an equal—equally frail, if you like—footing.

Return to your meditation on a continuous flow of experience, this time from the appearance aspect, using the interval between the breaths to take in the totality of the expanse of your awareness. From the perspective of your awareness, recognize the self as being constructed, let it shift in quality from palpably substantial to flickering animation, and take up the by-now-accustomed perspective of non-subjective natural awareness. With confidence in the stability of your concentration and your proficiency with pliancy, ease up a little to allow a little elaboration across the entire spectrum of your senses. Keep it light and barely effervescent. I was taught to adopt an inward orientation and see everything as in the mind, of the mind.[4] Instead of looking at things as they are, look at them as how they are appearing, how they are showing up in mind. Adopt a view of them as being an expression, a display of natural awareness.

You might find it helpful at first to take an incremental approach by attending to each of the five senses in turn, and recognizing the constructedness of their characteristic manifestations. But don't hesitate to take them all in at once. It can turn out that since they're no longer able to distract the self, they just end up involved with one another like children playing together in a make-believe world, oblivious of the parent, affectionately ignorable. Whatever scope of sense elaboration you open up to, always, always, always have it balanced against an unwavering and abiding engagement with the object of concentration, the eventing of the breath in the body, even as that object may come forth as little more than a bearing on your compass.

The next step is the easiest and the most fun. Relax your posture, open your eyes, stand up, and walk around. Maintaining your adopted view of all of phenomena as being constructed and your open disengagement with the senses, walk about in, look at, listen to, feel, taste, smell, and wonder at the world, continually allowing the whole business to show up as constructed. Take none of it as real; take all of it as cinematic. Keep this up for short intervals at first. The reactive self will still be primed to reemerge out of the background, take over the proceedings, and tip you into sentiment and imagination, in which domain you will be beyond instruction.

Cultivate direct recognition of the constructedness of everything your senses are displaying from the perspective of natural awareness. Direct recognition is the important part, not the enchanting side effects. As you gain experience, proficiency, and pliancy with this practice, the result will be that you come to experience the nature of things more than the specific fact of things.

Through practice with this meditation, starting out on the cushion, you should eventually be able to re-engage it at will during any of those many times in life when the self is disengaged, such as riding the bus, sitting in a park, or making your way through a crowd. With just an inflection, let the perception of you living your life go cinematic. Watch how the shift unweights the real. Pick up on the suffused sense of liberation that arises as you are relieved of everything you are bringing to bear. Recognize and affirm the lively expression of natural awareness. This isn't some idle pastime. You are incrementally softening the insistent coercion of your own perception.

Meditation II

The experience of dreaming provides a striking demonstration of the deluded way we designate phenomena as "real," as other than being constructed by natural awareness.[5] For a dreamer, the experience of a dream at the time of the dream is identical to the dreamer's waking experience of reality. The content of the dream, its objects and actions, and the dreamer of the dream, its subject, are taken to be "real." The self in the dream reacts as viscerally to that world as it would if that world were "real." When the dreamer awakens from the dream, the dream world evaporates as the "real" world re-emerges into "reality." The dream is recognized to have been not "real." From awake reality, the dream is recognized to have been a manifestation of mind.

Awakening from a dream creates the opportunity to recognize in your own direct experience not only that mind was constructing the dream, including your dreamed self, but also, if you pay close attention, that mind is, in turn, constructing what you take to be reality, including your awake self. The self is restored into its awake reality in one of the most magical episodes regularly experienced by a human being. In the first moments of waking, the urgent task of the mind is to orient you, to ground you in a time and place, to pin you down so that it can reassemble the rest of the world around a stable point. As "reality" re-emerges into "existence," you catch a fleeting glimpse of the constructedness of the world you take to be real. But that glimpse is just as instantly obscured by the anxious assertion of reality by the mind. That glimpse is the opportunity for insight.

IN THIS SECOND MEDITATION, we are going to adopt a view once again, and then watch as the experience of phenomena comes forth. The view in the previous meditation was phenomena-as-cinema, which tends to reinforce the sense of self *as* the observer. The view in this meditation is the more intimate phenomena-as-dream, where the experience of phenomena is viewed as it is unfolding simultaneously *with* the observer in non-subjective natural awareness.

In the previous meditation, you were looking at the film projection. In this meditation, you look at the dream. Return to your practice using the interval between the breaths to take in the totality of the expanse of your awareness. From the perspective of your awareness, recognize the self as being constructed, let it shift in quality from palpably substantial to merely constructed, and take up the by-now-accustomed perspective of non-subjective natural awareness, the context in which the self is being constructed. Ease up slightly to allow a little elaboration, light and barely effervescent, across the entire spectrum of your senses, and regard the totality of experience, including the experience of your self and your body, as a dream.

Regard each moment of experience, both its subject and its objects, both you and your world, as being dreamed, as being constructed by natural awareness, not corrupted by a notion of "reality." Look at the dreamlike quality of each moment of the experience of self and phenomena, of space and light, without allowing "reality" to develop. If solidity gets in the way, inspire yourself with the realization that, at the fundamental level of the least particles, all matter, including your body, is but an apparition to the torrent of neutrinos coursing unimpeded, voluminously and unceasingly, through the porous sieve we call reality.

After a few minutes with this view, let "reality" develop momentarily, and watch for the way in which the experience of this development parallels your experience of you and your reality emerging back into "existence" upon awakening from a dream. The experience of self-and-phenomena-as-dream shifts to self-and-phenomena-as-reality, with no change in content. Recognize that "reality" is just an attribute projected onto experience by mind. The "reality" of both self and phenomena, the dreamer and the dream, is being manufactured by mind. If the insight meditation into the constructedness of self hasn't already done so, this one should startle you with the recognition that awareness is not inside your skull.

What you have been regarding as the experience of an observer observing objective phenomena turns out to be the experience of the display of natural awareness constructing you and your phenomenal world, dreaming you and your world. When you look directly at the subject, content, space, and light of the phenomenal world, you are looking directly at the display of natural awareness. There is a single fabric here, a single nature, nondual.

To view the phenomenal world from non-subjective, nondual natural awareness is to step outside the anxious urgency with which the mind asserts the reality of that world. It is to step into a view where there is no difference in nature between the experiencer and the experienced. The nature of both is the lively expression of natural awareness. That display *is* natural awareness. Watch for the resolution of natural awareness into nonduality.

An important subtlety needs to be highlighted before you get too far along with this practice. The "phenomena-as-dream" description of the view for this meditation is a simile. Reality is not to be taken as an actual dream but as dreamlike. The dream world, while experientially and apparently mistakable for a real world, is missing the single most important characteristic of the real world: it is not a world shared with others. Only the dreamer experiences the dream world, and it vanishes upon awakening. The real world, ruthlessly enough, never does that. Every investigation into the nature of reality is meant only to undermine our delusions about the nature of that reality, the way in which we take it to exist. Whether or not reality exists in the absolute way we take it to exist cannot be determined from within mind and is, in any case, of no consequence to how we conduct ourselves in it.

WE ARE in a far more radical place now than we were with the constructedness-of-self insight practice. From natural awareness, the constructedness of self can have a dream-like quality, but now we recognize that all phenomena are also dream-like, also a manifestation of mind. It's not just appearance that's manifest by mind. It's everything we attribute to that appearance, not least its materiality. It does not follow that mind creates matter in the way in which we take it to exist—substantially real. Rather, the way in which we take matter to exist is a manifestation of mind.

Constructedness is not independent from the mind. Without making any decision one way or the other about the existence of relative reality, recognize that that reality, that quality, that nature is attributed to experience by mind. We're not trying to decide whether or not reality exists in the way we take it to exist. As practitioners, we are debating neither the apparent fact nor the moral moment with which relative reality is stuffed. We are concerned only with whether and how it might be possible to peel back the layers of reactivity to find the root of that reactivity, and thus the root of conduct.

Refine

Once you have some experience in practice with the constructedness of phenomena, there is a further refinement you can make that will acquaint you directly with the raw nerve of reactivity and, by implication, with the nature of the ground it obscures. This is a sophisticated refinement, so come back to it another time if it seems unintuitive to you just now.

To allow reality to develop, we have to allow ourselves to ignore the unified, nondual display in which experience is arising. We have to become ignorant. In fact, ignorance is our usual condition. It is ignorance of the nondual nature of each moment of experience as it arises that causes experience to be sundered into self and other.[6] From here, within our duality-soaked predicament, can the arising of experience be observed in its natural state before the entanglement of distorting constructions flares up? If so, what would that state be?

For the first meditation in this chapter, I wrote that your basis is still the imperturbable object of concentration: some incarnation of the eventing of the breath in the body, anything from physical inspiration to mere "moment-iness," little more than a bearing on your compass. From this basis, the meditation takes in a continuous flow of experience. But the knowing awareness of the eventing of the breath in the body, the object of concentration, has itself transformed into a continuous flow of experience. In doing so, it has dissolved into the continuous flow of all experience, and the continuous flow of all experience comes forth as both the object of concentration and the basis of meditation.

Concentration and meditation are no longer separate.[7] The eventing of the breath in the body still cues the shift to a continuous flow of experience, but thereafter, the knowing awareness of the continuous flow of all experience has all the hallmarks of the erstwhile object of concentration, even as it is the basis for meditation: calm, abiding, utterly spacious, and effortlessly self-sustaining. And all of this can be carried off the cushion.

In practice, set up the conditions for the unelaborated arising of all of experience by shifting to non-subjective, nondual natural awareness, and then attend to the very horizon from which the continuous flow of all of experience seems to be arising. Attend to that very first gesture of mind by way of which a thing becomes a thing. Any thing. The breath, the body, the self, space, light, any thing. As all of experience unfolds, stay with this very first impulse, the emergence of the particular out of the imminent. This will be a flickering process at first, since particularization immediately carries the moment away into "thingness."[8] By the time anything has any meaning, it's too late. But with practice, you will be able to stay imperturbably with just the imminent, since its native equanimity is self-reinforcing. Your liberation lies precisely in becoming thus, equanimous.

This practice of tracing the totality of experience, both the observer and the observed, back to the arising and disappearing from non-subjective, nondual natural awareness is meant to take you close to the world, not away from it. This is still the real world. Your view of it now is one of profound intimacy, from natural awareness.

With their relentless emphasis on "emptiness," traditional texts can seem at times to be extolling a condition of disengagement and abstraction that bears no resemblance to an engaged and compelling human life. On the contrary. What you may need to be wary of now is not of being taken in by the reality of reality, but of being overwhelmed by the beauty of its nature. If space-time is the fabric in which the universe takes place, natural awareness is the fabric in which space-time takes place. It is the realm of astonishment that shines forth as human experience trails away into its farthest reaches.

Meditation III

First, a gentle reminder to the reader that the following description of the direct-knowledge meditation into the constructedness of phenomena is meant to be evocative only. Unless your practice has already brought you here, read it simply for the sound of it, trusting that its sense will come another time.

With the two previous meditations, the emphasis was on working with the constructedness of phenomena from the perspective of natural awareness. With this direct-knowledge insight meditation, the emphasis will be on the awareness doing that constructing.[9]

In this version of the meditation on the constructedness of phenomena, you will refine and intensify the meditation by looking even more closely at the awareness that is doing the constructing, to see whether you can find the appearance aspect as an agent. You examine the appearance aspect of awareness directly for knowledge about the awareness constructing the experience of phenomena.

Specifically, in the continuous flow of experience from non-subjective, nondual natural awareness, you pick up on both the appearance aspect and the knowing aspect of that experience. You then pick out the appearance aspect, as you have practised and become familiar with doing, to see whether you can come to any conclusion about it, whether you can recognize it as having any basis.[10]

This direct-knowledge insight meditation on the constructedness of phenomena is, once again, a refinement and an intensification of the nature-of-experience meditation just described. Start from a similarly spacious perspective and eased-up presence, then pick up on the appearance aspect from the perspective of the awareness that is constructing experience across the entire spectrum of your senses, light and barely effervescent. Shift from the experience of the arising of appearance to the appearance aspect of the awareness that is the ground of that appearance. In the spectacular display of all of experience from the perspective of natural awareness, you are trying to spot the agent of that display, the appearance aspect itself. To throw that ground into relief, it can help to let the display elaborate and glitter a little, without getting carried away by it.

Without concept, without expectation, with ease, look nakedly, stare at the stream of experience, whether apparently continuous or apparently in discrete moments.[11] Inspect the stream of sprouting thoughts and emotions and perceptions to see whether you can find any basis for any of it. Recognize not just that awareness is constructing appearance but that the appearance aspect itself, to which we have been attributing the agency of appearance, is being constructed. Like gazing into flames in the night, there is a continuously arising blaze. With intensification, look only at the arising, and let appearance itself burn away, leaving no basis in its wake, leaving just the night sky. What is it that is blazing?

As before, this is not just a negating practice, a practice of negating the apparent reality of phenomena. It is an affirming practice as well: your experience of natural awareness resolves even more compellingly into nonduality. Natural awareness has the capacity both to know and to appear, without agency.

. . .

It is said that this direct experience of the constructedness of the appearance aspect of mind brings forth the true nature of natural awareness—like light, but with the capacity to know itself.[12] As Daniel P. Brown puts it, the appearance aspect just is:

> mind-as-appearance-itself shines forth. Its seeming coarse-level contents—perceptual aspects, thought, and emotions—just *are*. They are properties inherent in being human.[13]

By this point in the practice, you will be dialled right down to the mental atoms of the flow of experience, the unobservable moment before the emergence of a particle or a wave, as intimate with mind as you have ever been. The nature-of-experience meditations on the constructedness of the self and the constructedness of phenomena have laid bare the recognition that they are not different in nature. The mind is creating all of experience, not least its subjectivity and its materiality.

In turn, the direct-knowledge insight meditations on the constructedness of the self and the constructedness of phenomena have laid bare the recognition that what we have been designating as the knowing and appearance aspects of awareness themselves have no basis. To this refined experience of natural awareness, with its now cleared-out aspects of knowing and appearing, you can bring intensity to look closely at the current upon which these aspects are borne. Look directly at non-subjective, nondual natural awareness to see whether you can spot the arising of the river of knowing and the river of appearance, which you are now free to watch as they flow by.

Look until you recognize that the discrimination of awareness into a knowing aspect and an appearance aspect, as handy as it has been so far for practice purposes, collapses as you become intimately close to the flow of natural awareness.[14]

The moment of knowing co-occurs with the moment of appearance. They are inextricable. Whenever you are tempted to take the knowing and the known as different—which most of your practice so far has had you doing as a result of the artificial distinction between appearance and knowing—recognize that this too is a construction. In an inevitable reconciliation, these two will be recognized as one and the same: self-aware, self-illuminating natural awareness.[15] The knower and the known give rise to each other. The knower and the known are one and the same. They fall away into natural awareness, which, it is said, is like space and like light, but with the capacity to know itself.

Resolution

In summary, the resolution of natural awareness into nondual natural awareness, like the original emergence of non-subjective natural awareness, can be sudden and striking, or it can be the gentlest dissolution of a gossamer thread of constraint. It can show up in a flash or be so surreptitious that you don't recognize it until you are in the midst of it, until someone points it out to you. It will be accompanied by an unmistakable sense of liberation, which you may experience viscerally or emotionally, but also perhaps without a lot of fanfare. Insight is often like this—a remarkable shift that occurs in the most quotidian way. When the veil between the knower and the known slips away, the "you" you thought you were becomes more permeable to all of what you experience as reality. All of experience is nondual natural awareness reflecting itself to itself. This is a theoretical statement at this point; you don't have to take any of it on faith. The insight practices are intended to create the opportunity for you to recognize these qualities for yourself.

You will frequently encounter evocative adjectives such as "clear" and "luminous" in descriptions of nondual natural awareness. You will need to remind yourself again and again, as I do, that these terms are allegorical, and clumsy, at that. Don't look in a visual sense or any other way for clarity or luminosity. These descriptions are not about how things truly are; they're about how to *recognize* how things truly are. They are prompts for the recognizing mind. When recognition arises, the only resemblance it will have to these adjectives is a poetic one, corresponding to what you recognize in only the most abstract way.

In my experience, luminosity is akin to encountering a turn of phrase I've never heard before but which, uncannily, almost predictably, renders some experience I've had for which I have never found words. What I had fully felt but been unable to express is thrown into full view, full light. And in my experience, clarity is akin to almost casually, even accidentally, happening upon the now obvious and deeply simplifying solution to some persistent conceptual problem in which I had been absorbed. Everything becomes clear in something of a collapse.

But these are conceptual allegories of the experience of luminosity and the experience of clarity. In the context of insight, in neither case is the experience conceptual, and in neither case is the experience subjective.

You may protest to your teacher, after much practice, that you would describe what you have come to recognize in different language than your teacher's, and it will be your teacher's recognition of your description for what it is that will let you know you are describing the same thing. We use language because it's the best we have. The recognition and knowledge you are after, however, simply do not lie within its reach. Don't look in any way. Set up the conditions for nondual natural awareness to show up by not elaborating anything in experience. The affirming part always arises from its own side.

Undecidability

The assumption of the reality of reality, the materiality of reality, is so fundamental that there's none more fundamental. Most descriptions of the world are riddled with endless, intricate ontological debates, the passion of which is to determine that an objective reality either does or does not exist. The heat of these debates comes from the very different consequences for being human that would result from deciding one way or the other. Provoking them are a couple of commonplace observations.

First, it's possible, experience being the interior thing it is, that my experience of the colour orange, say, is not at all like yours. If I could experience what you experience when you see orange, I might see green. If we were both looking at an orange, we'd both be experiencing what we would each call "orange"; we would both be seeing an orange orange, but yours would be green to me if I could share your interior experience. From within mind, we can't even verify whether the experience of colour is in common.

Further, take Mongolia, for instance. You can show it to me on a map, you can tell me what you know of it, you can show me photos of it. But these are all representations of Mongolia, not Mongolia in fact. While it's out of sight, is it only out of mind? What does it take to re-establish Mongolia in experience, and what state is it in until then?

From within mind, the evidence for the reality of the bulk of the universe at any given moment is anecdotal. As you swing the beam of your attention around in the world, in what way is everything outside your attention real? It's real by memory, by consensus, by habituation and predictability. But these are symptoms of reality. From within mind, we have a tiny scope within which we feel we can unquestioningly verify the reality of reality. The continuity of all the rest of it in time and space is left to a kind of statistically-based trust. The corroboration of the reality of everything outside the immediate mists over. Our minds are not crammed with an extant reality, they are crammed with sustaining an alleged reality.

WHETHER REALITY DOES or does not exist in the way we take it to exist is undecidable from within mind. I'm choosing the word "undecidable" because it resonates with some of the imagery and poetry I find in traditional instructions for this insight practice. The traditions' response is to say that what we take to be reality neither exists nor does not exist. What are we to make of this contradiction?

The opposite of this contradiction—the abstract assertion that something either exists or does not exist—derives its incontestable truth from an intolerance of contradiction. To allow contradiction to be true would destroy logical truth. Contradiction derives all of its falseness from the threat it poses to truth. The falseness of contradiction is the clinching rivet in the closed logic of what we call knowledge. It is a declaration of the bounds of knowledge.

That boundary constrains us to the domain of either/or, to the imperious dictates of bivalence. If we presume only the possibility of either knowing or not knowing, we shut ourselves into decidablity. Being the measure of all things, no matter in which direction we turn, we will only ever be greeted by our limitations.

The traditions' response—that what we take to be reality neither exists nor does not exist—is not a statement of either ignorance or incapacity. It's not an ambiguity or an ambivalence; it's a positive acknowledgement of the latency of all that lies outside the bounds of what we take to be knowledge. The latent is the field out of which what we take to be knowledge gets carved.

Undecidability is not an impairment or a deficiency; it's an attribute of the larger context within which knowledge as we have construed it is circumscribed. Undecidability makes the shift to regarding contradiction as a way of knowing beyond the barrier shutting in the domain of either/or.

To say that reality neither exists nor does not exist is not to say, "We don't know one way or the other"; it is to say, "This *is* the way we know this."

To decide that things exist condemns us to reactivity. To decide that they don't is a craven evasion, both foolhardy and dangerous. To allow reality to neither exist nor not exist is to acknowledge the limits of knowledge at the frontier with the latent. The latent is the expanse that unfurls when the rigid clamps of either/or are sprung.

That expanse may evoke in us a sense of mystery or wonder, but it is neither of these things. That expanse is the necessary accompaniment, the matching ground to the figure of knowledge. This background lets us know the foreground is a relative contrivance, and in so doing, announces the potential for our freedom.

THE INARTICULATE BEAUTY of these meditations on the constructedness of phenomena is that they free reality from the constraint of either existing or not existing. They free your experience of reality from the constraint of being merely real, and they reveal to you that your experience of reality is being constructed. Even as it is ever this old world, moment to moment, this is just a possible world.

14
TIME

There is no single time: there is a different duration for every trajectory; and time passes at different rhythms according to place and according to speed. It is not directional: the difference between past and future does not exist in the elementary equations of the world; its orientation is merely a contingent aspect that appears when we look at things and neglect the details.... The notion of the "present" does not work: in the vast universe there is nothing that we can reasonably call "present." The substratum that determines the duration of time is not an independent entity, different from the others that make up the world; it is an aspect of a dynamic field. It jumps, fluctuates, materializes only by interacting, and is not to be found beneath a minimum scale.

— CARLO ROVELLI

The intent of the nature-of-experience insight practices into the constructedness of self and the constructedness of phenomena, in their commonplace contemplative forms, is to expose to us the vulnerabilities of our assumptions about how things are. In their evocative meditative forms, their intent is to get us to catch the thievery of those assumptions as they arise in our minds and steal away our freedom. The remarkable thing about these practices is that they take relative reality itself as the vehicle for liberation. Relative reality comes forth as it always has and always will, but when everything in each moment carries with it insight into the nature of itself, then each moment is an opportunity for liberation. Nothing has changed, and everything has changed.

However, the description I just gave contains a further entanglement: the entanglement of time, with which the word "moment" is burdened. In the quotation opening this chapter, we have an eloquent physicist working at the frontier of quantum gravity telling us that for all the qualities we attribute to time, no basis for it can be found in relative reality. Rovelli's observations, though, as wonderfully undermining as they are, hesitate at the last moment: while they question the qualities we attribute to time, they leave intact the fundamental assumption that there is an actual reality of some description that we experience as time. This assumption is at once the most deeply ingrained and the most elusive of the three aspects of relative reality that the nature-of-experience insight practices seek to expose.

Once your practice evolves to the point where you can stay continuously with the undifferentiated flow of the eventing of the breath in the body from non-subjective, nondual natural awareness, you are in a position to unstitch the vestigial restraint implied in the phrase "undifferentiated flow," the restraint of your ordinary sense of time. If you aren't there yet, let what I describe here by way of practice and insight stand in for the open ground you will eventually traverse yourself.

Meditation I

The commonplace version of this meditation is to observe conceptually that your entire sense of time occurs in the present, sometimes referred to as "the now" but in no way deserving of the definite article. When you think of the past, all you are doing is animating a present memory. Bundled up in that memory is a quality of pastness, but the memory itself is occurring now. If you take that memory as evidence that time occurs as you take it to occur, you're relying on the flimsiest of evidence. The evidence of memory is concocted, unreliable, and shifting. The evidence of memory is good evidence that the experience of the past is a constructed experience, and that the construction of that experience is an ever-novel recreation in the present.

The future is an even more rickety construct. The past gains currency by being construed from experience and pervading the present. The future, construed as it is from nothing but projections, doesn't have a leg to stand on. The past seems continuous with the present. The future is just a big blank that shows up out of nowhere. With a term such as "daydreaming," we overtly acknowledge that the future is a reverie. The only thing that can be agreed upon is that disagreement about it will be universal. By the time the future shows up, it can't be distinguished from the present. At no point in time does it exist. When you think of the future, you are painting in the air. Nothing lands; nothing sticks. The medium itself vanishes, and it does so because it's made of thought, a construction of mind in the present.

Recognition of the constructedness of both past and future in turn makes nonsense of the notion of the present, "the" now. The present is defined as that which is between the past and the future, which vanish upon inspection. The present is approached infinitely in the infinitely narrow gap between the past and the future and is never reached; a vanishing thing between two other vanishing things. It's the mind that gets in there and makes something out of nothing.

This meditation is more than just a thought experiment. It will not merely entertain with its conceptual provocations. It will unsettle your experience of time. When conducted with a light touch, stable focus, and adequate duration, it can occasion momentary dropouts in your self-satisfied sense of continuity. This experience is excellent preparation for the next two on-the-cushion practices, and it travels well; you can do it on the bus, if you like.

Meditation II

Take up your usual calm-abiding practice on the cushion from the non-subjective, nondual perspective of natural awareness, and carefully and gently let surface your sense of the reality in time of "yesterday," "today," and "tomorrow," each in turn. Attend as little as possible to their content. Attend instead to the sense you have of pastness, now-ness, and future-ness. Let the character of each emerge for you in your direct experience—a sense of what has happened, what is happening, what will happen—until the temporal sense of them is stronger than any content.

When you ignore content, how is your sense of the past fundamentally different from your sense of the future? Stay in the company of this experience of the mere character of the past and the future, let them flatten and subside in power before you confront the more intransigent distinction you're attributing to the present. If the present is a feature of time, how does it fit between the past and the future? If it has a duration, that duration must have a beginning in the past and an end in the future, leaving us no further ahead. If it has no duration, how can it be present?

The present is a dimensionless potential away from which the past and the future extend, and in so doing, they wipe it out. Attend to the way you douse each fissile moment with the dross of recollection and the dead weight of expectation.

THE MORE YOUR temporal sense of each of these three attributes of time is teased out from the designations you are giving them, the more they will have in common—that temporality itself is attributed by mind. When this recognition is held closely and for long enough, the constructedness of these attributes will come forth and surreptitiously unfetter you. Keep this up, alternating gently between the constructedness of past and present and future until the distinction between them fades as their common constructed nature comes forth, and you are left sitting with a beginning-less, duration-less, endless experience, the experience of atemporal natural awareness.

These instructions are designed to bring you to the recognition of the true nature of the seeming reality of time—its constructedness—in a way that leaves you in the world as you ever were, and the world as it ever was, with the difference that time, like you and the universe you inhabit, is known to be appearance.

Meditation III

As with the first two nature-of-experience insight practices, the third form of the meditation on the constructedness of time presents the opportunity to refine and intensify your practice so that you chase time into the thin air that it is.[1] The refinement is to drop your attention below even the constructedness of arising, staying, and ceasing, below the horizon at infinity, whence they are spawned. As always on this path, something is deconstructed and something is affirmed.

The traditional instructions for this meditation are utterly elusive.[2] I can, of necessity, have little to say, and certainly nothing instructive. They require that you discriminate the flow of experience into discrete moments to provide a context in which a beginning, a continuing, and an ending might be sought. They require you to adopt a view, a way of looking at these moments "as if" they had no beginning, no continuing, no ending. And they require you to maintain a radical absence of conceptuality or expectation, a transparent receptivity to spontaneously arising, always-here natural awareness that only turns up with a complete cessation of searching.

On the page, they are simple, direct, even flat-footed. Their haiku-like sparsity should tell you that their message is nowhere to be found in the words; it's entirely interstitial. When heard in meditation guided by the voice of experience, they are incantatory. The chemistry of these instructions, the insight they evoke, will only arise in the presence of the appropriate reagent: a practitioner abiding calmly in self-knowing, self-illuminating natural awareness.

Where self-knowing and self-illuminating describe what natural awareness is *like*, always-here describes how natural awareness *is*: imminent.

Imminence

With this insight practice, any expectation about what remains once time as an experience starts to empty out instantly impairs recognition of the nature of that ground. Description does not just fail; it actively obscures. In language, even the most stolid noun is shot through with temporality, and the most fleeting adjective can never escape duration; but let's do what we can with a noun made out of an adjective: imminence.[3]

I'm choosing this word because it resonates with some of the imagery and poetry I find in traditional instructions for this insight practice. It's as slight a word as I could come up with for the experience of ever-present natural awareness that glints and flickers into view with this practice. Imminence is the motionless gesture out of which all temporality—and everything else—emerges. If undecidability is an attribute of the matching ground to the figure of knowledge, then imminence is the glow of that ground, its off-put—or, as my teacher Susan Mickel puts it, "the empty fullness of potentiality." All that can be said about it by way of instruction is that you will know it when it shows up.

If the insight practices into the constructedness of phenomena open into the realm of the undecidable, these into the constructedness of time open into this realm of bare imminence, the liminal pause out of which the experience of time emerges. Imminence is not of no duration. It is outside of duration, unfettered by duration. It simply inheres.

The resolution of time into imminence is not a mystical experience of something beyond, something other than you already know. It's an experience of the nature of time from which you have never been apart. Time itself is showing you its nature.

Something motionless and duration-less might be taken to have collapsed in on itself, a plunging, all-consuming singularity. But that impression arises from coming at imminence conceptually. Encountered instead from natural awareness in all its non-subjective, nondual, atemporal expanse, imminence can be experienced as a namelessly resplendent presence, one without a sense description, a "–ness," flaring with creation.

. . .

Until now, I have been using "constructedness" in place of the traditional term "emptiness," but here at last is the essence of emptiness. With this final shift of natural awareness into its quintessential manifestation, we have come upon its most significant attribute: natural awareness alone in all of experience is unconstructed. Here at last, the traditional descriptions of emptiness are the only possible words.

It is said that natural awareness is beyond words and concepts. It is uncreated, non-existent, and unceasing. It has no centre and no edge. It is self-knowing, self-illuminating. It is unbounded in capacity. It is the groundless ground of being. It is empty.[4]

PART IV
RETROSPECT AND PROSPECT

15
PRACTICE

> Perhaps instead it is us, and our interactions with the universe, that are particular. We are the ones who determine a particular macroscopic description.
>
> — CARLO ROVELLI

We have covered a lot of territory. However, compared to putting all of this into practice, this has been a swift and superficial survey. We started with a review of the tools with which you are endowed: your body in all its wondrous sensibilities, and your mind in all its world-making manifestations. You built your concentration practice upon an elemental set of six practices I think you will find always have something more to teach you, no matter how experienced you become with them.

To create the opening for insight practice, you were introduced to the notion of perspectives—provisional views to take up, not because they are actual destinations, but rather to enable particular practice experiences. These perspectives were couched in a broader framework describing experience, mind, and awareness, and the appearing and knowing aspects that permeate them.

With the resulting language in hand, you made your way through the nature-of-experience insight practices, thereby resolving your experience of awareness into its original nonsubjective, nondual, atemporal nature. The sole purpose of this resolution into natural awareness is to liberate you from the snare of reactivity woven into the delusions we all share about the nature of reality.

Along the way, you were asked to consider alternatives to some of the certainties with which, out of anxiety, we protect ourselves, and upon which, predictably enough, we impale ourselves. These alternatives included regenerative interpretation in place of stifling orthodoxy, speculative undecidability in place of ontological neurosis, and the spontaneity of imminence in place of the chains of causality. These are not just attendant topics. They are the indications that throughout practice, you must be prepared to question your way of knowing, and, for your liberation, you must be prepared to forego its reassurances.

Throughout this book, I have emphasized the importance of grounding your practice in compassionate motivation, rounding it out with visualization and self-invocation, and extending it into your life by carrying it off the cushion. There have been what I hope are helpful words about teachers and students, about the tyranny of metrics, and about the unflinching arbiter of authenticity: recognition in your own direct experience.

While I have pointed to the inextricability of wisdom and compassion, I will be the first to admit that this presentation has been lopsided in its focus on the path of wisdom, to the neglect of the path of compassion. This is not to undervalue the path of compassion but rather to provide a complement to the many available presentations of compassion practice that tend not to elaborate upon the path of wisdom in the kind of detail you've seen here.

THIS TREATMENT of the calm-abiding concentration and insight practices has emphasized their empirical basis. All of these practices consist of methods to apply and outcomes to observe. Even where the descriptions of the outcomes test the limit of words, an experienced and skilled teacher can still recognize the state of your practice. As your practice evolves and you start to hear your fellow students ask questions you once asked, and you anticipate and understand the meaning of the teacher's response, you will see that these practices trace out a terrain native to and latent in the human experience. Countless traditional practitioners have traversed this territory time and again, and they have enshrined their knowledge within the traditions in the form of these practices.

In addition to stressing the empirical basis for these practices, I have repeatedly reinforced the principle that only you know how to find your way. A teacher can work with you to corroborate what you are up to and indicate possibilities to explore, but the choice of how to develop your practice must be yours alone. When others around you recount enviable journeys, or you are tempted by allegedly privileged teachings, you may have to lash yourself to the mast of your own skill with recognition to find your own path with self-respect, discernment, and authenticity. With these practices, you have a complete foundation upon which to establish a habit of practice in your life and to extend it into the nature-of-mind practices when the time comes.

Throughout both contemporary and traditional writing on practice, you will encounter unabashedly evocative descriptions of meditative experience. These descriptions are hard to avoid due to the very nature of that experience, and they can be profoundly inspiring at just the right time in your practice. But they are not the goal. They are an ephemeral part of the path, good indicators that you are heading in the right direction, but not to be counted on to show up, let alone to validate your practice. They are side effects of insight, not insight itself. These experiences are best absorbed into your being and never exposed to the dissipating light of publicity. Whatever your experience, keep your practice focused on recognition, and deepen that. The hallmark of experienced practitioners is how little they have to say about experience. Instead, they conserve every ounce of their being for the only outcome of practice that matters: compassion and equanimity in everyday life.

As DIVERTING as the nature-of-experience insight practices can be as thought experiments, it's essential to bring their meditative forms to your practice on the cushion so that recognition of them in your direct experience explicitly disentangles you, little by little, from a lifetime's habit of reactivity. Recognition changes how you are. This transformative outcome deepens and becomes more subtle with the nature-of-mind insight practices. These take the mind itself as evidence, and they take a blunt and immersive approach that you may by now be out-of-the-way enough to be susceptible to. For you to be able to benefit from them, you must have recognized and be open to the power of traditional teachings, and you must hear them in the full wisdom and compassion of the voice of a lineage teacher.

From here on, there are few autodidacts. There's an immense and diverse body of works you can read, but they are likely to come across as inscrutable or insubstantial if you have done nothing to cultivate an ear for them. Some are held close to the chest by the traditions, not so much because they are secret or dangerous, but because it would be a waste if they were to come to you before you were able to hear them. Others will dovetail perfectly with the foundations you've established here and can carry you onwards for years to come.[1]

And this is only the beginning. What we have covered here is but one approach to just the fundamentals of practice. Not only are there many other approaches—there is an enormous treasury of traditions and practices that take the exploration of being and knowing into deeper, more exquisite, and more mysterious territory than can be touched upon in a single human life, and all of it for the sake of the liberation of all beings.

Never forget

The single most important practice is never to forget your predicament: never forget that you are estranged from your own true nature, and that this estrangement is the root cause of the snare of reactivity. The bulk of liberation lies in this recognition. The rest is nurturing something raw but otherwise already whole and complete. If this awareness of your predicament is somewhere in the back of your mind at all times, echoing faintly in passing moments or barking out sharply in critical episodes, then every moment is a moment of practice.

The traditions are replete with knowledge, wisdom, understanding, hard-won experience, and an unwavering commitment to the propagation of compassion for all beings. But this will all be lost without practitioners such as you. You bring to this endeavour the miraculous treasure of your body, your innate capacities for calm abiding and insight, the unplumbed depths and unmined gifts of your astonishing mind, and the silent tracking of that unannounced questing of the heart that brought you to these practices and through them. These practices create nothing new. They reveal what you already have, how you already are. They are the crucible that resolves the alloy into its elements.

At the centre of practice is the assertion that relative reality, this life, *is* your practice. There isn't anything that isn't rising up to greet you. There isn't anything that isn't an opportunity for liberation. This is all home. Finding your own way is a moral imperative; nothing else will serve authenticity. Dedication is rooted in unchoosing everything towards which your reactivity is strategized, and compassion is the effortless balm into which your reactivity can dissolve.

THE QUOTATION at the head of this chapter speculates on whether the way forward might not require an acknowledgement of an exclusively subjective universe. If you bring to this speculation any degree of recognition of the constructedness of subjectivity itself, it turns into the proposition that the knower and the known are one and the same. Perhaps one day, the ultimate Nobel Prize in Physics will go to those who demonstrate that when science and insight practice seem to be on common ground, it is not because they are looking *at* the same thing, but because they are looking *with* the same thing.

Relative reality is a sleight of hand, an apparition arising from the ground of being, and this life itself, silting particulates in the sunbeams of that creation. But the extent to which reality is a sieve is also the extent to which it is a web. The porousness of relative reality entails the obliteration of discontinuity. The outstanding feature of what's left of what we take to be reality turns out to be its undivided interconnectedness.[2] There isn't anything that isn't a part of everything. That interconnectedness is the compassion that is the very nature of the ground of being.

These foundational practices and all that follows from them are based on the conviction that realizing your true nature is an ambient liability. All you have to do is expose yourself to it. In fact, it's amazing it hasn't already occurred to you. Your liberation is inescapable.

Compassion

I suppose the question is, do you want to live superficially on the familiar surface that reality-as-we-take-it-to-be presents, or do you want to live from the depths of your being? To wave the question off, you have to smother the way your unsettled heart mourns the loss of the ground it once knew. If you are untroubled by such a shadow, you're all done. But if the question strikes a chord, these practices are here to take you where you need to go. They demonstrate that reality-as-we-take-it-to-be—once you let its nature shine through in everything, everywhere, at all times—is itself the vehicle of your liberation.

Even as they disentangle you from the relentless cycle of your reactivity, these practices replant you in this life lived here, now, as it is. You can count on two things then. The wonder of being will saturate everything, without you being able to say anything about it; what you come to know will manifest instead as how you are. And you will have every opportunity to become the most capacious conduit you can possibly be for compassionate conduct to arise in this world of its own accord. Practice turns out to be a way to become a part of the beginning of the flourishing of peace.

. . .

One spring evening, I went to catch the Third Street train to go downtown to hear a concert. It being the middle of rush hour, I knew the train would be full, but when I boarded, I spotted a seat right by the door. I sat myself there beside a young couple with their daughter between them, occupying the rest of the bench. They also were dressed for an evening out.

The four of us were facing into the train, and in front of us was a rough pack of teenage boys, jostling and punching one another, laughing and shouting at one another. I realized I could thank them for the seat I was in having been vacant. They were in the throes of the searing energy and attendant vulnerabilities of adolescence, desperate to outplay it all with swagger and bluster. Something of the loneliness I sensed in their bravado had me wondering whether some of them might be fatherless.

In their heedlessness, one of them lurched into the face of the little girl seated between her mother and her father beside me. Just in time, the father blocked the boy's impact with an outstretched arm, protecting his daughter. In response, they laughed and leaned in on us aggressively, sneering and violent, before backing off and resuming their gritty banter with one another, leaving the little girl terrified and on the verge of tears.

Whatever sympathies I had for them were swept away. Instead I found myself feeling angry and threatened, trapped in my own starkly racist reactions. An unremarkable evening was now bristling with tension. I was casting about in my mind, trying to decide whether and how to defend, escape, or ignore in return. I didn't like any of my options. I couldn't think what to do. I could make no decision. The only thing of merit I was doing was staying calm, patient, and careful.

And then, without a thought, I watched myself as I turned toward the family beside me, smiled at them, and struck up a conversation. Turning sideways towards them, I had angled my shoulder into the aisle but without bumping into any of the boys. At my greeting, the whole family seemed to edge up along the bench into the crook of my other arm resting along the back of the bench behind the father. Their three faces formed a single gaze, fixed on mine.

I asked them what event they were off to, and whether they were going out for dinner beforehand. I didn't feel particularly kind or protective, just engaged and civil. They asked the same questions of me, and we all chatted quietly for a bit, my outside shoulder still firmly set into the aisle, and no more boys leaning into us. I had a vague sense that they may even have become a bit subdued. I and the family kept looking directly at each other as we exchanged small talk. I think we all knew what we were doing for one another.

A few stops later, we arrived at a major transfer point, where the boys piled off in a reckless crush, and just as the train door was closing to separate them from us at last, they spat stringy gobs of snot at us. One messy one landed on the father's shoulder, but mother and daughter were untouched, and they were proffering tissues for the father to clean his coat with. Still turned toward them, I felt someone touch my own shoulder from behind. I turned to find a woman offering to wipe off the gobs of snot I hadn't realized had landed on the back of my own coat.

As she was carefully cleaning them off me, I glanced down the train car through the rush-hour crowd. To my amazement, I saw that every face there was turned toward us, open and engaged, every one of them with us, level and present. I realized then that they had all been there as we had made our cocoon as a foursome.

They had all shown up without being called upon. They had all been in the same jam as I, trying to decide what to do. The way it had unfolded had somehow brought us all together, quietly and without fanfare. For just a moment, I saw none of us as closed off into selves. For just a moment, I saw all of us as embodied compassion.

I was the first to disembark. I bid the family good evening, as grateful to them as they were to me. I glanced along the train one more time at all those strangers who had been transformed into fellow human beings simply by having shared mutual care and concern for a few minutes one spring evening, and I stepped off the train. I felt at peace, not so much with myself as with all of us on that train. I was aware not of what we had done, but of what we had become. The outcome had unfolded on its own and left us all undamaged and whole. No winners, no losers. No violence countered, but none created, either. That's all.

I REALIZE that the communal cocoon excluded the boys, and that the wall shutting them out was built upon the lack of courage and conviction in my compassion for them. I know there must have been an even more resolving outcome that would not have left even that barrier in place, that would have included the boys, and that it was my own entanglement with my own reactivity that prevented it from flourishing.

So, acknowledging the distance still to go, I turn back to practice and the road ahead.

DEDICATION

To the memory of the remarkable
Thupten Kalsang, the Rahob Rinpoche,
with profound gratitude.

AFTERWORD

I realize you have taken a risk attending to the words of someone whose own practice is still evolving, and who has no credentials whatsoever as a teacher. Where I may have been reckless, even transgressive, I hope you will take it as a sign of the eagerness I have for the task I set myself.

I can only find what I have written here wanting compared to the direct experience I have been attempting to describe. I can no longer hear what it is I would have said if I had written this as it was unfolding for me then, as I hope it is unfolding for you now. Hindsight is a liability to the description of a journey, but I had no idea I would write about this particular journey until I was looking back on it.

I cannot always be certain whether what arose in my own direct experience did so in its own original way, or whether it arose to meet the story I was being told. More critically for you the reader, I cannot always be certain of where what I have written here is an account of my own journey, and where it is instead that story telling itself. There's nothing I can do about this; it's the way with words.

I live and write in a privileged, White, Western context. As a result, what I have to say here about the potential of compassionate conduct may come across as naive and elitist to the disenfranchised, to those whose voices are unheard or discounted. I can offer only that my intent has been to describe a path of practice informed by an alertness to, and a wariness of, the ways of power.

I could not have *not* written this book. I had to write it to free myself from its words, to cast off the moorings of its sentences, to let the sails of my practice catch the wind, fill out, and carry me off into the life I am meant to live.

I live in the thick of a bonded social web animated by a passion for endeavour, commitment, and human love, none of which is much addressed by the traditions. If these entrench me in my predicament, so be it. All I ask of my practice is that it should enable me to live with compassion and die with equanimity.

I hope what I have written here lands for you in language and from a perspective that resonates with your own. I hope it contains something that will move you to take up practice, but also that disarms you enough to approach the traditions on their terms without in any way compromising your own.

I have had the extraordinary benefit of patient, insightful, generous teachers, all of whom respect orthodoxy but none of whom are bound by it. In this they display the most arresting confidence that these teachings can withstand even the ministrations of an uninstructed worldling. You have shown great heart in picking up this book and reading through it, and I fervently hope you too may find such teachers, and that your practice will unfold broadly and unceasingly, freeing you in every moment.

IN MEMORIAM DANIEL P. BROWN
1948 - 2022

The Student, the Teacher, and the Woods: A Bedtime Story

Once upon a time in a far-away land (in April of 2005 at Esalen on the Big Sur coast), there was a Student in the Woods. The Student was clambering about in the Woods, he had been in the Woods for some time, he was adept in the Woods. One day, the Student came upon a Teacher. Now this was a confident Student, confident enough that he felt he'd had enough of teachers for one lifetime. Just the same, he asked the Teacher, "What are you doing here?"

"I'm on my way to a Clearing over there," replied the Teacher. Now the Student knew his way around these Woods, and while he'd heard of Clearings, he'd never seen one, and certainly not in these parts. So he asked the Teacher, "Which way are you headed?" in reply to which the Teacher pointed out an obscure, illogical, unpromising Path. The Student gave it one look and told the Teacher he thought it was an obscure, illogical, unpromising Path. The Teacher shrugged off the Students protests, said "Well, I'm off," and went on his way leaving the Student standing there in the Woods.

Now the Student, being a confident Student, thought these events over, thinking to himself that he was perfectly comfortable in the Woods, he always knew where he was and where he was going, so a little side-trip to have a look at an alleged Clearing could do no harm. And since he knew there were no Clearings in these parts, it would be a chance to prove to himself the Teacher had been talking through his hat.

So the Student set off down the Path which proved to be steep and confusing and often dark, and the Student tripped on roots, banged his head on low-hanging branches, scraped his knees on the rocky terrain, and stumbled at last, a bit worse for the wear, into a Clearing. As he dusted himself off, he looked about the Clearing and, small though it was, could not help but admire the setting, uncluttered and quiet. He spotted the Teacher waiting there for him, casting an impatient glance at his watch. "Come on," said the Teacher, "There's no time to hang around here, you still have a long way to go."

Now it certainly came as news to the Student that he was on his way anywhere, but something unusual about the Clearing gave him pause. He considered that perhaps he didn't know everything there was to know about the Woods, that now he was in the Clearing, he might not have been the complete woodsman he had always thought himself to be. Not only that, but now he was stuck here on some Path with this guy! So he asked the Teacher "Now which way are you headed?" The Teacher pointed out another obscure, illogical, unpromising Path. The Student gave it one look and told the Teacher he thought it was an obscure, illogical, unpromising Path. The Teacher shrugged off the Students protests, said "Well, I'm off," and went on his way leaving the Student standing there in the Clearing.

The Student stood a while in the Clearing where he felt faintly at home, and after a little more thought tinged with resignation, set off down the Path after the Teacher. Now this Path also proved to be steep and confusing and often dark, and the Student tripped on roots, banged his head on low-hanging branches, scraped his knees on the rocky terrain, and stumbled at last, a bit worse for the wear, into another Clearing, this one a little more expansive than the first. He spotted the Teacher waiting there for him, casting an impatient glance at his watch, now also tapping his foot, giving the Student the impression he'd had quite enough of the Student's protests. "Come on," said the Teacher, "There's no time to hang around here either, you still have a long way to go."

"I'll get there when I get there," grumbled the Student to himself, but the Teacher had already turned and headed off down another obscure, illogical, unpromising Path.

So this somewhat dysfunctional, but quite productive relationship (productive for the student at any rate, we have no idea what kind of grief it caused the Teacher) between the somewhat grouchy Teacher and the somewhat defiant Student continued in like fashion for some years until one day (in December of 2011 in Boston), the Teacher brought the Student to the edge of a Lake. Now Clearings the Student had heard about, but not only had he not known this Path would lead him to a Lake, he hadn't even known there was a Lake. He was standing there in moderate astonishment, looking at the Lake lying Clear and Calm at his feet when the Teacher said, "Come with me now out onto the Lake." Now the sharp-eyed Student was not to be taken in. He spotted that preposition, and he protested, pointing to the Water at his feet saying "But, but, but …"

The Teacher looked down at the Water, looked back at the Student in perplexity and said, "It's only Water, what's your issue?" Once again, the Student turned to the Teacher to protest, but this time when he looked at the Teacher, he saw the Teacher had changed.

There were the same blue eyes, and there was the same pugnacious set of the jaw. There were the same elfin Instructions and tart replies. But something was different. For one thing, the Teacher thought a lot more things were funny than he had before. But the Student also noticed a light happiness hovering about the Teacher, he was faintly effervescent, just beaming stuff straight at the Student. He gave the Student an Instruction that was Simple and Clear and Perfect, and it went *thmmmp* right into the Student's solar plexus. And before our now unguarded Student could say anything about anything, he realized he had stepped out onto the Lake.

With this we come to the end of this chapter in the ongoing story of the Student, the Teacher, and the Woods, but as we all head home to our sleep and our dreams, we can cast one last look back at the Student standing there with his Heart broken wide Open, and we can all Listen as the Teacher whispers in the Student's ear, whispers in all our ears (in a familiar Boston accent), "If you think this is something, just you wait until I take you to the Ocean."

ANNOTATED BIBLIOGRAPHY

Calm-abiding Concentration Practice

TRADITIONAL SOURCES

Dalai Lama XIV, and Chodron, Thubten. *Following in the Buddha's Footsteps.* Boston: Wisdom Publications, 2019.

"Chapter 7: Obstacles and Antidotes: The Nine Stages of Sustained Attention" presents a succinct, contemporary presentation of the nine-stages pedagogy. The book itself, the fourth in the multivolume *Library of Wisdom and Compassion* series, lays out a daunting 552-page curriculum, but you can find this five-page excerpt in the Summer/Fall 2019 edition of *The Wisdom Journal*, on pp. 8–11 in the print edition, and on pp. 5–6 in the digital edition online at: www.wisdomexperience.org/journal (accessed 21 January 2026).

Dharma Fellowship. "Deepening Calm-Abiding – The Nine Stages of Abiding." web.archive.org/web/20230703052041/www.dharmafellowship.org/library/essays/nine-stages-of-abiding.htm (accessed 21 January 2026).

Tibetan Buddhist Society Melbourne. "Nine stages of concentration." www.tibetanbuddhistsociety.org/nine-stages-of-concentration2/ (accessed 21 January 2026).

> Both of these are concise and complete presentations of the nine stages, with explanations of all of the symbols, including the elephant, the monkey, and the rabbit.

The literature by traditional teachers on the nine-stages pedagogy comprises its canonical presentation, but it is not an easy read. In each of the following references, the cited chapter can stand on its own. That might be the best way to approach them until you are more acclimatized to the traditional vernacular.

Lodrö, Geshe Gedün. *Calm Abiding and Special Insight*. Ithaca: Snow Lion Publications, 1998.

> "Chapter 4: Nine Mental Abidings" presents the single most comprehensive treatment of this topic, although it is more than a little convoluted. The following two references don't expand much on what you'll find here.

Rinbochay, Lati, and Rinbochay, Denma Lochö. "Chapter 4: Calm Abiding," in *Meditative States in Tibetan Buddhism*. Boston: Wisdom Publications, 1997.

Thrangu, Khenchen. "Chapter 3: Identifying Experiences in Śamata Meditation," in *The Practice of Tranquillity and Insight*. Ithaca: Snow Lion Publications, 1993.

CONTEMPORARY SOURCES

The traditional texts on concentration practice cited above can strike the modern reader as encumbered with practised archaism, more formulaic than expressive. In looking for more contemporary voices, you will be disappointed. This traditional pedagogy for calm-abiding concentration practice, in spite of its renown, its availability, and its efficacy, has been broadly ignored by the popular, highest-profile, bestselling books that purport to teach contemplative practice. Instead, most such books, in their relentless pursuit of happiness, give concentration practice a cursory chapter or so, sometimes even just an appendix, before expounding on some version of insight practice for which you will be ill-prepared.

On the other hand, the two popular, high-profile, bestselling titles cited below provide much useful practical information about concentration practice, but they do so in the context of idiosyncratic descriptions of states and metrics, and questionable models of mind and consciousness that can only exacerbate exactly the kinds of concretizing conceptual tendencies from which determined practitioners are struggling to dis-impair themselves.

Don't let any of that delay you. Just pick out the advice about actual concentration practice techniques, and make them work for you. Read for what will add depth and momentum to your practice, then get back to what you were doing.

Wallace, B. Alan. *The Attention Revolution*. Boston: Wisdom Publications, 2006.

> Handily enough, you can winnow out the best the book has to offer by sticking to those sections the author himself has titled "The Practice."

Yates, John. *The Mind Illuminated*. Pearce, AZ: Dharma Treasure Press, 2015.

Insight Practice

TRADITIONAL SOURCES

Khenpo Tsultrim Gyamtso Rinpoche. *Progressive Stages of Meditation on Emptiness*. Ynys Graianog, UK: Shrimala Trust, 2016 (also Auckland, New Zealand: Zhyisil Chokyi Ghatsal Publications, 2001).

This is a transcription of oral teachings given by Tsultrim Gyamtso over a number of years to different audiences in a variety of venues. It is organized variously into stages of practice, stages of realization, and schools of thought, as well as into a history of traditional understanding as a progression of increasingly subtle teachings. The content covered here is just the first two stages (pp. 1–61, pp. 1–44 in the 2001 edition).

I am stopping shy of the final three stages in the book, since together they present the evolution of the two great contrasting views on the ultimate nature of reality within the traditions. These views are differentiated from each other by a vanishingly subtle epistemological distinction that has, nevertheless, not prevented the one from accusing the other of nihilism and the other accusing the one of eternalism, and kept both of them writing at it for a thousand years. So, more than we have time for just now.

CONTEMPORARY SOURCES

Brown, Daniel P. *Pointing Out the Great Way*. Boston: Wisdom Publications, 2006.

> This is at once a wide-ranging survey, an ambitious synthesis, and an intricate exegetical analysis of a dozen or so renowned traditional root texts and commentaries. In addition, the critical approach taken is a semiotic one known as semantic field analysis, occasioning many scholarly dilations. While the result does not stint on the arcana, the balance of delicate intricacy with an expansive scope is something to behold.

Burbea, Rob. *Seeing That Frees*. West Ogwell, UK: Hermes Amāra Publications, 2014.

> This is the book that I most want to leave you with. It assumes you have a foundational practice such as is described here, and it opens out into widening and deepening insight practice. While it's based on sources from within the most ancient of the traditions, it is respectful of the full range of traditions and is something of a reconciliation of them. It emphasizes practice in a contemporary lived life, and it is secular in its approach. Not only does it offer a broad range of practices, it also offers a sustained arc of practice that lifts you as it unfolds. Nothing is left uninspected. There is only one insight, and that is "emptiness." There is only one outcome, and that is liberation. Each stepping stone along the way is exposed as a contingent support for the next, as the journey winds its way to the groundless ground of being.

Approaching the Traditions

Batchelor, Stephen. *Buddhism Without Beliefs*. New York: Riverhead Books, 1997.

> A resolutely secular book with which to first acquaint yourself with the roots of the traditions, perhaps precisely because it's a self-consciously revisionist one.

Dzogchen Ponlop Rinpoche. *Rebel Buddha*. Boston: Shambhala Publications, 2010.

> An excellent portrait of what practice looks like in a lived life, especially the section on transcendent action.

Karr, Andy. *Contemplating Reality*. Boulder: Shambhala Publications, 2007.

> A concise and comprehensive, if credulous, practitioner's guide that provides a sound foundation for learning and reflection, and for navigating the entire traditional path of practice.

Yongey Mingyur Rinpoche. *In Love With the World*. New York: Spiegel & Grau, 2019.

> A beautiful and compelling account of practice in a lived life. Simultaneously a remarkable story and a comprehensive teaching.

NOTES

2. Tools

1. For a succinct guide to the classical "seven-point" posture, see Kathleen McDonald, "Posture: A guide to the seven-point posture," *Tricycle* (Fall 1995), www.tricycle.org/magazine/mind-body (accessed 21 January 2026).
2. For some latitude in the classical posture, see Rochester Zen Center, "How to sit," www.rzc.org/get-started-zen/how-to-sit (accessed 21 January 2026).

3. Capacities

1. See Brown, *Pointing Out*, "The Stages of Concentration," 277–283.
2. A good explication of *The Elephant Path* and its symbols can be found at www.tibetanbuddhistsociety.org/nine-stages-of-concentration2/ (accessed 21 January 2026), and a beautiful and classic rendering of it can be found at www.columbia.edu/itc/hs/tibetan/tibetanciv/maplib/tiles/e999c46b-d24797a17b045f53261e3153/14798bc9190173.jpg (accessed 21 January 2026).
3. See "Calm-abiding Concentration Practice" in the Annotated Bibliography.
4. For the most succinct and contemporary description of these stages, see Dalai Lama XIV and Thubten Chodron, *Following in the Buddha's Footsteps*.
5. See Dharma Fellowship, "Deepening Calm-Abiding – The Nine Stages of Abiding," web.archive.org/web/20230703052041/www.dharmafellowship.org/library/essays/nine-stages-of-abiding.htm (accessed 21 January 2026).
6. In Brown, *Pointing Out*, "Basic Skills for Contemplation and Meditation," 153–157, these skills are described as "directing, intensifying, pliancy, and intelligence." Here I have expanded "directing" into "placing and staying," and "intensifying" into "refining and intensifying," and I have added the pair "releasing and spaciousness" based on my own experience being taught these skills. I have addressed "pliancy" and "intelligence" as "pliancy" and "metacognitive awareness" in parallel with all six skills.
7. See Brown, *Pointing Out*, "pliancy," 155.

4. Placing and Staying

1. See Brown, *Pointing Out*, "Protecting," 145–150.
2. See Brown, *Pointing Out*, "intelligence," 153, "full awareness," 156.
3. See Brown, *Pointing Out*, "ability to stay," 156.

5. Refining and Intensifying

1. See Brown, *Pointing Out*, "Intensifying," 240.
2. For another version of this exercise, see Brown, *Pointing Out*, 154.
3. I am indebted to my teacher George Protos for this particular formulation.
4. I am indebted to my teacher Susan Mickel for this particular formulation.
5. See Brown, *Pointing Out*, "mind-moments," 229.
6. Referred to as "laxity" and "excitement" in Lodrö, *Calm Abiding*, "dullness" and "flightiness" in Brown, *Pointing Out*.
7. See Brown, *Pointing Out*, "dullness and its opposite, flightiness," 203.
8. See Lodrö, *Calm Abiding*, 78 and 83, respectively.
9. For a similar analogy, see Brown, *Pointing Out*, 155.
10. See "Calm-abiding Concentration Practice" in the Annotated Bibliography.

6. Releasing and Spaciousness

1. See Tsoknyi Rinpoche, *Carefree Dignity* (Hong Kong: Rangjung Yeshe Publications, 1998), "That constant movement is how the mind works," 39.
2. See Brown, *Pointing Out*, "Mistakes Become Wisdom," 371.
3. See Burbea, *Seeing*, "Modes of Insight and 'Ways of Looking'," 32–33.
4. See Brown, *Pointing Out*, "subtle dullness," 241, "subtle flightiness," 250.
5. See Dalai Lama, *Following*, 2019

7. Knowingness

1. See Gyamtso, *Progressive Stages*, "two aspects," 31 (21 in the 2001 edition).
2. See Gyamtso, *Progressive Stages*, "there is always something knowing," 31 (21 in the 2001 edition).
3. See Brown, *Pointing Out*, "event-perspective," 286.
4. See Brown, *Pointing Out*, "mind-perspective," 286.
5. See, for example, Burbea, *Seeing*, "awareness of awareness," 132.
6. The traditions themselves disagree as to whether or not experience actually occurs in discrete moments, so feel free to take either the continuous flow or discrete moments as the object of concentration; just be sure the

perspective is from the knowing aspect. See Brown, *Pointing Out*, 497, note 277.
7. See Gyamtso, *Progressive Stages*, "the division … is a conceptual invention," 41 (28–29 in the 2001 edition).
8. The two best-known nature-of-mind practices are Nyingma Dzogchen and Sarma Mahāmudrā, huge topics beyond the scope of this book.

8. Practice

1. See Wallace, *Attention Revolution*, and Yates, *Mind Illuminated*.
2. See Gyamtso, *Progressive Stages*, "Feeling," 27 (18 in the 2001 edition).
3. See Christina Feldman, "Dependent Origination," *Insight* (Spring 1999), 37–42, www.buddhistinquiry.org/article/dependent-origination/ (accessed 21 January 2026).
4. For an exhaustive and subtle, book-length treatment of this most fundamental of traditional topics, see Rob Burbea, *Seeing That Frees*.
5. See Gyamtso, *Progressive Stages*, "the ignorant moment of consciousness," 52 (37 in the 2001 edition).

9. Text

1. See, for instance, the remarkable study of the bible as literature in Northrop Frye, *The Great Code* (Toronto: Penguin Books Canada, 1990) and *Words with Power* (Toronto: Penguin Books Canada, 2007). In their expansive humanism, these books demonstrate that criticism can be the salvation, rather than the discrediting, of scripture.
2. For a similar derivation of suffering as a consequence of reactivity, see Burbea, *Seeing*, 89, in the discussion of the fabrication of "dukkha."
3. See Gyamtso, *Progressive Stages*, 1–61 (1–44 in the 2001 edition).

10. Stages

1. See Brown, *Pointing Out*, "three stages," 285.
2. See Gyamtso, *Progressive Stages*, "Three Stages," 5 (1 in the 2001 edition).
3. For a concise analysis of these topics in the Western tradition, see Jan Westerhoff, *Reality: A Very Short Introduction* (Oxford: Oxford University Press, 2011), and for a typically exhaustive (if resolutely partisan-Gelug) traditional analysis, see Khensur Jampa Tegchok, *Insight into Emptiness* (Boston: Wisdom Publications, 2012).
4. See Gyamtso, *Progressive Stages*.
5. See Brown, *Pointing Out*, "serviceable," 152.
6. See Burbea, *Seeing*, "Chapter 25: Emptiness and Awareness (2)."
7. For an in-depth traditional presentation of the complete path of learning and reflection, see Karr, *Contemplating Reality*.

11. Insight

1. See Gyamtso, *Progressive Stages*, "stages in the development," 11 (6 in the 2001 edition).
2. See Gyamtso, *Progressive Stages*, "shine forth unimpeded," 6 (2 in the 2001 edition).
3. See Gyamtso, *Progressive Stages*, "Relative Truth" and "Absolute Truth," 9–10 (4–5 in the 2001 edition).
4. Burbea, *Seeing*, 32.
5. See Brown, *Pointing Out*, "concentration at an optimal level," 290.
6. See Brown, *Pointing Out*, "affirming negation," 301.
7. The background to these first two types of meditation can be found in Gyamtso, *Progressive Stages*, 15–61 (1–44 in the 2001 edition).
8. The background to this type of meditation can be found in Brown, *Pointing Out*, "Chapter 6: Special Insight," 283–360.
9. See Tsoknyi Rinpoche, *Fearless Simplicity* (Hong Kong: Rangjung Yeshe Publications, 2003), "These two are inextricably interconnected," 21.

12. Self

1. For a characteristically insightful elaboration of this point, see Burbea, *Seeing*, "Respecting the Self," 107.
2. For a penetrating and nuanced eleven-page essay on the constructedness of the self in general, and the aggregates in particular, see Burbea, *Seeing*, "Chapter 11: The Experience of Self Beyond Personality."
3. See Gyamtso, *Progressive Stages*, "The five skandhas," 26 (17 in the 2001 edition).
4. Burbea, *Seeing*, 37.
5. See Tsoknyi Rinpoche, *Carefree Dignity* (Hong Kong: Rangjung Yeshe Publications, 1998), "natural awareness," 46.
6. See Brown, *Pointing Out*, "something still remains, namely the mind's natural awareness," 301.
7. See Gyamtso, *Progressive Stages*, "Feeling," 27 (18 in the 2001 edition).
8. This phrase looks forward to the "let be" idiom prevalent in Dzogchen nature-of-mind texts such as Tsoknyi Rinpoche, *Carefree Dignity* (Hong Kong: Rangjung Yeshe Publications, 1998), and Tsoknyi Rinpoche, *Fearless Simplicity* (Hong Kong: Rangjung Yeshe Publications, 2003).
9. See Brown, *Pointing Out*, "a step toward understanding the real nature of the mind," 179.
10. See, for example, Burbea, *Seeing*, "Chapter 29: Beyond the Beyond."
11. See Brown, *Pointing Out*, "awakened wisdom" and "special insight," 283–284.
12. Based upon "Emptiness of the Person" in *Pointing Out*, 292.
13. See Brown, *Pointing Out*, "locate the basis of the mind," 295.
14. See Brown, *Pointing Out*, "the mind by the mind," 296.
15. See Brown, *Pointing Out*, "the potential to know itself," 305.

16. Brown, *Pointing Out*, 306.
17. This quotation appears near the end of the beautiful essay on the relationship between concentration and insight in Burbea, *Seeing*, "Chapter 5: Samādhi and Its Place in Insight Practice," 60.

13. Phenomena

1. See Brown, *Pointing Out*, "concentration at an optimal level," 290.
2. See Brown, *Pointing Out*, "optimal balance," 294.
3. See Brown, *Pointing Out*, "A refined level of calmness is no longer needed," 314.
4. See Brown, *Pointing Out*, "inward orientation," 311.
5. See Gyamtso, *Progressive Stages*, "The Dream Example," 44 (31 in the 2001 edition).
6. See Gyamtso, *Progressive Stages*, "klesha mind'" 52 (37 in the 2001 edition).
7. See Dakpo Tashi Namgyal, *Moonbeams of Mahāmudrā* (Boulder: Snow Lion, 2019), "the unification of śamatha and vipaśyanā," 93.
8. For more on this refinement, see "Child Viewing a Temple" in Brown, *Pointing Out*, 265.
9. Based upon "Emptiness of Phenomena" in *Pointing Out*, 309.
10. See Brown, *Pointing Out*, "All these ... are understood to be non-existent," 315.
11. See Brown, *Pointing Out*, "look nakedly," 315.
12. See Brown, *Pointing Out*, "the capacity to know itself," 317.
13. Brown, *Pointing Out*, 307.
14. See Brown, *Pointing Out*, "nonduality collapses the distinction," 308, "mind-as-appearance-itself shines forth," 307.
15. See Gyamtso, *Progressive Stages*, "self-illuminating, self-aware mind," 49 (35 in the 2001 edition).

14. Time

1. Based upon "The Yoga of Unelaboration" in *Pointing Out*, 342.
2. See, for instance, Pema Karpo's root instructions, quoted in Brown, *Pointing Out*, 347–348.
3. To be carefully distinguished from "immanence," with its Deist overtones.
4. See Tsoknyi Rinpoche, *Carefree Dignity* (Hong Kong: Rangjung Yeshe Publications, 1998), "Mind essence ... is empty in a different way," 41.

15. Practice

1. See in particular *Seeing That Frees*.
2. See Brown, *Pointing Out*, "interconnectedness of everything," 357.

www.ingramcontent.com/pod-product-compliance
Lightning Source LLC
Chambersburg PA
CBHW020903080526
44589CB00011B/411